**by Elizabeth Levy**

**with Additional Material by J. R. Havlan**

**Illustrated by Daniel McFeeley**

**Originally published as *America's Horrible Histories***

SCHOLASTIC INC.

New York   Toronto   London   Auckland   Sydney
Mexico City   New Delhi   Hong Kong   Buenos Aires

To Philip Winn for all his help.
—E. L.

**Expert Reader:** Professor Forrest McDonald, Distinguished Research Professor of History, University of Alabama

0-590-12250-9

12 11 10 9 8 7 6 5 4 3 2 1     2 7 3 4 5 6 7 8/0
Printed in the U.S.A.                    40

First printing, July 2003

www.ElizabethLevy.com

# Contents

# Funny But True

*History is usually a random, messy affair. . . .*
Mark Twain, *A Horse's Tail*

*The one who tells the stories rules the world.*
Hopi saying

**S**ometimes the funniest things are true. George Washington loved his hound dogs so much that he named them Truelove and Sweetlips. **America's Funny But True History** is about just this kind of real, factual, *funny* history. Being able to laugh is not only a good way to get through the day, it's really a wonderful way to learn.

There's a saying that if you don't know your own history, you are condemned to repeat it. I say that if we can't laugh at ourselves, we're in even worse trouble. Human beings do odd, strange things; no one people has a monopoly on making mistakes. History is all about real lives and real people—and these same people often loved to tell a joke. If you can share a joke, it's hard to hate.

There are facts and jokes in this book that will make you laugh out loud, some that will

make you grin and groan, and others that will make you squirm. While you're laughing at all the jokes and cartoons in *Revolting Revolutionaries,* remember, the information in this book is true, at least as far as anybody knows.

My best teachers were always the ones who could laugh. One wonderful teacher, my rabbi, once told me that nobody can ever know the whole truth, but that it's worth holding on to those little slivers of truth that we do find. It's hard to find the truth in history. There is always new historical information being discovered that gives us new ways of looking at history. Historians keep learning and ideas about what really happened in the past change as quickly as most people change their underwear!

**T**homas Jefferson once wrote, "No one of us, no, not one, is perfect." Maybe that's why I love this period of history. The men and women of the American Revolution knew they weren't perfect. They were brave, brilliant, crabby, scared, and foolish, often all at the same time. Many of them wrote down practically everything they did. That's why we know so much about the Revolutionary War.

The American Revolution lasted eight long, rough years, from 1775 to 1783. In many ways it was a family fight. The British thought of the American colonies as their children. The Americans thought they were grown up enough to manage their own affairs, especially their taxes. Family fights are nasty. Feelings get hurt. Family fights stink, sometimes literally. The American Revolution was quite smelly. Soldiers were ordered not to take baths. Baths were supposed to be unhealthy and might make the soldiers too relaxed. Most soldiers had fleas. Fleas are *not* relaxing!

Were the revolutionaries really revolting? Yes, but not if you mean disgusting. To revolt comes from a Latin word for turnover. To revolt means to turn or change the way you live. It's not easy to think about the world in a new way. It takes guts to actually change the way you live. You need great courage to risk dying for change.

But was change possible? Could people really live without a king or queen? Most Europeans and American colonists would have said no before the American Revolution. Could a big country be a democracy? "Never," said almost everybody. The few democracies in history had been in small countries and none had lasted very long. A big country where people elected their own leaders? A democracy? America was too big, it was crazy to try.

Still, on a cold day in January 1776, George Washington raised a flag for his rebel soldiers with 13 red and white stripes on it, one for each colony that revolted against England: Georgia, South Carolina, North Carolina, Virginia, Delaware, Maryland, New Jersey, Pennsylvania, New York, Connecticut, Rhode Island, New Hampshire, and Massachusetts.  Nobody thought the 13 British colonies would ever unite about anything. Virginians hated New Englanders, and New Englanders felt the same about them. Almost everybody hated New Yorkers.

On July 2, 1776, the 13 colonies officially claimed their independence from England. "All Men are created equal," Thomas Jefferson wrote in the Declaration of Independence. The rebels pledged their sacred honor and their lives to "the united States of America." There had been no such place as the United States of America on July 1 — and then there was.

Not everyone in the colonies wanted independence, not by a long shot. In fact, the revolutionaries never really were a majority; they were only about a third of the population. Most likely another third were loyalists who stayed loyal to the king. The loyalists wanted the revolution to fail. Everyone else tried to stay neutral. Many families were split in two about the war.

Of the estimated 30,000 Americans who fought in the Revolutionary War, about 5,000 were African Americans who fought side by side in the front lines with white colonists.

The leaders of the Revolution and the writers of our constitution were men, but women played an important role, too, in the birth of our country. You can find out all about our founding fathers and mothers in the sections called "Meet the Parents."

Thomas Jefferson was right. Our founders weren't perfect — they *were* revolting! They changed the way the world thinks and lives. The dreams of democracy they gave to the world are still not complete. But Americans keep trying to fulfill those ideals and that may be one reason the nation has lasted.

Elizabeth Levy

# Hello, loyal readers!

Mel Roach here. No doubt you recognize me from previous books. You'd be surprised how often I hear that. In fact, since I became the official tour guide for America's Funny But True History, I've been so busy signing autographs and posing for pictures, I've barely had time for my all-time favorite activity: exploring the farthest reaches of your kitchen cabinets in search of tiny pieces of stale, rotten food I can eat for breakfast. (You're probably thinking, "Now, that's revolting!")

But enough about my highfalutin lifestyle; it's time we learned a little more about these "revolting revolutionaries." Like our nice author, Elizabeth, just said, America in the 18th century was full of many brave and independent men and women (and kids!) who just wanted their own space. It's like finally

**Mel Roach** in person today

getting your own room, but in this case it's a whole country! That's a lot of responsibility (not to mention a big place to keep clean!).

So let's turn the page and see how those revolutionaries did it. And keep an eye out for me as you read. After all, I am a roach — and I have a habit of popping up when you least expect me to. Happy revolting! . . . I mean, "reading"!

# Chapter 1
# The Revolution: The Prequel

**R**ight before the American Revolution, the population in the 13 colonies exploded. In 1700, the colonial population was only about 250,000. Seventy-five years later, in 1775, it had increased ten times, to 2.5 million. One myth about the colonies is that most Americans were poor compared to rich Mother England. Nothing could be further from the truth. Most Americans, even the poor ones, lived better and ate better than their cousins in England.

**TIME LINE**

**1754 to 1763**
French and Indian War

**1760**
George III crowned King of England

**1763**
Pontiac's Rebellion

# A Snapshot of Colonial Life

Who came to British colonial America? Not many of England's aristocrats. It was mostly the lowborns, the adventurers, and the troublemakers who wanted to go. The new Americans came from all over Europe, not just England. Only about 60 percent of the white colonists were from England itself. The rest came from Scotland, Ireland, Germany, Holland, and many other countries.

Then there were the half-million Americans who came in chains from many different countries in Africa. They were sold as slaves. Most lived in the South, where they worked the tobacco plantations and rice fields. But slavery was legal in all the northern British colonies, too, and many white families in the North owned slaves. A few wealthy New Englanders, mainly in Rhode Island, made money from the slave trade.

The wealthy colonists loved to show off. Instead of private airplanes, they had private coaches drawn by four horses whose color had to

**1765**
Stamp acts; Sons of Liberty founded

**1770**
Boston Massacre, Massachusetts

**1773**
Boston Tea Party, Massachusetts

match. They dressed themselves and even their servants and house slaves in silk outfits. The rich loved to dress up. They wore silks, velvet, and lace.

There were lots of fights and battles between the small number of rich families and the big majority of poor ones. Rich and poor did have one thing in common, though. They loved to gamble. Colonial Americans would bet on anything: where a fly would land in a tavern, whether the gray or the tan horse would win a race. Boxing matches were fought without gloves and biting was allowed. Both the upper and lower classes played card games. George Washington loved to play cards, but his journals show that he was rarely lucky. And everyone loved a lottery.

## Read All About It

The 18th-century American colonists were the best-read people on Earth. Almost everyone could read the Bible. They gobbled up newspapers and especially news about England. In New York and Philadelphia alone, 2,000 ships arrived each year carrying news from all over the world. The well educated often read the ancient Roman classics in Latin. They also knew their law, particularly English law.

Educated Americans might read about the rest of the world, but a lot of the world turned up their noses at the Americans. No matter how rich Americans got or how well read they were, the British pretty much sneered at their cousins in America. The British thought that the Americans could never get their wigs right and that their dances were too rowdy.

But that didn't stop Americans from keeping up with the latest philosophies and newfangled ideas that were coming out of Europe. New ideas were in the air. The 18th century was a time of great scientific experiments and advances in the study of natural laws.

## Long Live the New King!

In 1760, England got a new king. George III took the throne and he looked good. For his coronation, George was dressed in an ermine robe and a jeweled crown, the same one the monarch of England wears today. The colonists read all about the coronation. Just like today, Americans loved news about the royal family.

## Meet the Parents

### Benjamin Franklin
### (1706–1790)

One person who grabbed new ideas out of the air was Benjamin Franklin. He flew a kite in Philadelphia and helped discover the laws of electricity. In one experiment, Franklin tried to cook a turkey by giving it an electrical shock. Instead, he almost electrocuted himself and was knocked out cold. When he came to, Franklin said, "What I meant to kill was a turkey. Instead I almost killed a goose."

Ben Franklin could make fun of anything, especially himself. He was a scientist, diplomat, inventor, and politician. He was a grade school dropout, but he taught himself to read Latin, French, Spanish, Italian, and German. He would study anything. He always loved to swim and studied different ways to be a good swimmer. Franklin also loved fresh air. He claimed that his long life was partly due to the fact that he gave himself an "air bath" in the nude almost every day. Franklin's scientific experiments and inventions, such as bifocals and the Franklin stove, made him the most famous American in the world.

# The French and Indian War: Au revoir!

When George III took the throne, everything looked peachy keen in his kingdom and in his colonies in America. England was winning a war in the colonies and getting ready to kick the French out of North America. That war was called the French and Indian War, even though the war was between France and England, with Native Americans fighting on both sides.

In 1753, the French owned Canada and claimed the entire Ohio River Valley. But many people in the British colonies wanted that land for themselves. War broke out and it lasted for nearly 10 years. During the French and Indian War, several of the American rebels who would fight in the Revolution got their first taste of battle, including George Washington, who wrote, "I have heard the bullets whistle and believe me there is something charming in the sound."

In 1763, the French lost the war in North America to the British. France gave up Canada and all of its territory east of the Mississippi River to England. It gave its territory west of the Mississippi to Spain to keep it out of England's hands.

THE BULLETS Whistle
all the hits from the 1760's

George Washington raves, "CHARMING!"

# Meet the Parents

### George Washington
### (1732–1799)

George Washington's father was a Virginia farmer who owned slaves. He died when George was 11. George's mother was a big woman who smoked a pipe and scared almost everybody who met her, especially George's friends. She cut off branches from peach trees and used them to swat George and his brothers and sisters on their bottoms and legs. She complained a lot. Even after Washington became president, she never once said she was proud of him.

By the age of 16, George was already six feet tall. All his life he loved going on wild gallops, hunting with his dogs that he gave names like Truelove and Sweetlips. His big, gentle hands and steady voice could calm any steed. He was just a teenager when he put on a uniform for the first time and fought for the British in the French and Indian War. He carried himself like a soldier from that time until the day he died.

Washington was a very brave man and also very proud. He hated to have anyone slap him on the back and pretend to be his buddy. He didn't show his emotions often, keeping himself in check like the soldier he was. But, at times, he could fly into a rage or break down in tears when a soldier he loved died in the war.

Spain immediately began trying to make sure it had a hold on the territories. The Spanish built their first Catholic mission to convert Native Americans in San Diego, California, in 1769.

**Mount Vernon** in Virginia was George Washington's home for almost his entire life. The farm is kept going just like it was in Washington's time.

**Mission San Diego de Alcalá** in San Diego, California. This mission is known as the "Mother of the California missions." Today, its gardens and white adobe church provide a little oasis just a short walk away from the NFL football stadium where the San Diego Chargers play.

## Deadly Games

For most Native Americans, the French defeat in America was a disaster. The French had treated them better than either the Spanish or the English did. Most tribes had been allies of the French. In 1763, Pontiac, the great Ottawa chief who had fought for the French for ten years, tried to unite all the tribes of the Ohio and Mississippi valleys to kick out the British colonists. Pontiac's Rebellion was brutal on both sides. In one battle in Michigan, Pontiac's warriors pretended to play a game of lacrosse outside a fort. When a ball went into the fort, the players stormed in, grabbed guns, and slaughtered all the soldiers, eventually cooking up a particularly fat man.

The British and colonial troops were just as brutal fighting back. At one peace conference near Fort Pitt (now Pittsburgh, Pennsylvania), General Jeffrey Amherst suggested giving the Native Americans blankets and handkerchiefs that had come straight from a smallpox hospital. Amherst's idea, which would have been an early form of biological warfare, was rejected for fear of infecting British troops. However, an epidemic of smallpox did break out at Fort Pitt, killing 60 to 80 Native Americans in the area.

During Pontiac's Rebellion, more than 2,000 white and black settlers lost their lives, and countless Native Americans died (literally countless because nobody kept count of how many of Pontiac's warriors were slaughtered).

George III and his government decided that it would be easier to make peace with the Native Americans than to keep fighting them. To their credit, George III and his government thought the Native Americans were now British subjects and that they deserved at least some protection. Parliament decided to forbid colonists from going into the western lands for a little while. Most

It's true. No matter what you do, English food is just bland.

colonists didn't think the Native Americans should get any protection. They just wanted to go in and take their land.

## Big Mama Stamps Her Foot and Wants to Be Paid

Britain was now broke. Keeping British soldiers in the colonies to protect the frontier cost money. The French and Indian War had left a national debt of 146 million pounds (British money). Parliament decided to try to get the colonies to actually pay their taxes. It wasn't that the colonies had never been taxed before. It's just that before there had been a lot of ways to get around taxes. Merchants like rich John Hancock in Boston were used to smuggling their goods past customs inspectors who could be bribed to look the other way.

In 1765, the British Parliament passed what it thought was a tiny little tax, called the Stamp Act. All newspapers, pamphlets, and legal documents, including birth certificates, marriage licenses, every deck of cards, even every pair of dice had to have a government stamp. The stamps cost money. All the money from those stamps went straight to England. Americans loved their games and hated to pay a tax on dice and cards. Almost everybody hated the new tax and they let the king know about it. The women went into the protest business, too.

## Knit One for Liberty

Seventeen girls and women got together in a house in Providence, Rhode Island, and organized one of the most successful protests against

*I owe taxes already? I just got here! Suppose I can't pay. What are they going to do, send me back?*

## Meet the Parents

### John Hancock (1737–1793)

Every rebellion needs a few million-aires to help finance it. The Boston rebels had John Hancock. Hancock wasn't born rich. He was an orphan who was adopted by his rich uncle. He inherited his uncle's business of import-ing tea, wine, and other things from England. Hancock soon figured out how to bribe the tax collectors so he didn't have to pay taxes. He was called the "King of the Smugglers." Hancock was as proud as a peacock and dressed like one, too. His favorite color was purple. But as much as he loved being rich, he ended up spending most of his fortune supporting the American Revolution.

the Stamp Act. They vowed not to wear British wool but to spin and make their own clothes. The London cartoonists made fun of them, but the women stuck to their knitting needles and spin-ning wheels. Women, who were mostly left out of political life, felt excited that finally they were needed. Women poets spread the word and so did men urging that women lead the way. The boy-cott spread as far south as the Carolinas and to all the colonies in between. Never before had female Americans formally been given a public role, and now they led the way. British merchants soon began to complain that they were losing their best customers. The boycott became one of the most powerful weapons in the American Revolution.

## It's a Riot — But It's Not Always Funny

Poor people couldn't vote, but they did have a way of making their politics known: They took to the streets and protested. The Stamp Act caused riots. Today, if you get in trouble with your teacher or your parents they might threaten to "read you the riot act," which means behave — or else! The phrase comes from an 18th-century law that said if a mob gathered, someone had to read them the law (the Riot Act) that gave them an hour to go home. Anybody still in the mob an hour later could be flogged (a fancy name for whipping) 39 times and given a year's prison sentence.

In the colonies, the mobs often didn't care if someone read them the Riot Act. They wouldn't go home. To protest the Stamp Act, rioters sometimes burned stamp collectors in effigy. An effigy is a fake body made of straw and cloth.

The protests against the Stamp Act got loud, loud enough that the king and his ministers heard about them in London. Nowhere were the riots noisier than in the harbor towns of New

York and Boston. In New York City, an angry mob of 2,000 sailors and apprentices marched on the governor's home on Bowling Green. They hanged and burned a straw effigy of the governor and then set his carriage on fire. The riots in Boston became more famous than the ones in New York. Boston had one thing New York didn't. Boston had the Adams family.

## Good Politics Needs Good Names

"It's good politics," wrote Bostonian Sam Adams, "to put and keep the enemy in the

Window smashers? Check.
Trash can burners? Check.
Rock throwers? Check. Runners/screamers? RUNNERS/
SCREAMERS??? It's so hard to get those guys to focus.

**When Riots Had Rules**

## Meet the Parents

### The Adams Family

### Sam Adams (1722–1803)

Sam Adams was a failure at everything he tried in his life — except revolution. Sam drove his family's brewery almost out of business. He tried to be a newspaper publisher and failed. He had gotten a job as a tax collector and failed so badly that he owed about 8,000 pounds in back taxes. He was also one of the world's sloppiest dressers. He walked around Boston in shabby clothes, with his big Newfoundland dog, Queue. Sam Adams might not have been good at making money, but he was very good at making friends. Both Sam and Queue were welcome in taverns all over Boston. Everywhere Sam Adams went he listened to the complaints of the workers and sailors that he met and he never talked down to them. They liked him. Sam Adams was a genius at what people today call networking.

### John Adams (1735–1826)

John Adams, Sam's second cousin, was a revolutionary leader, the nation's first vice president, and then the second president of the United States. He always wanted to be famous and he got his wish, but he wasn't always well liked. Short, stout, and kind of testy, he was a poor country lawyer, living outside Boston when the struggles with Britain began. He was looking for a cause that would give him a "bold push" into the world. "Will it be quick — shall

I creep or shall I fly?" he wrote in his diary. He devoted his life to pulling the colonies together in order to win the fight against England. Of all the rebels who wrote about their lives, John Adams's accounts are perhaps the most fun to read, because he didn't lie to himself, and he included all the gossip about whom he disliked and why.

## Abigail Adams (1744–1818)

Abigail Adams, John's wife, was just 15 when she met her future husband. She had educated herself in her father's library. John Adams's first impression of her wasn't very nice. He thought Abigail wasn't very "frank or candid." But he came to realize that first impressions are often wrong.

During their five-year courtship, Abigail began calling John her "dearest friend." They married in 1764. For 10 years (1774–1784), while John Adams served in Philadelphia in the Continental Congress, Abigail raised and educated five children and managed the family farm in Braintree, Massachusetts. She and John wrote each other almost every day. Their letters make the early history of our country come alive. Abigail Adams spoke her mind in her letters. She wanted to abolish slavery and wanted Congress to expand the rights of women. Neither happened during her lifetime.

My Dearest Friend,
Could you hit the Piggly Wiggly on your way home? Pick me up some pectin, tallow, ambergris, and do get the dry-cleaning.
Love, Abigail

**Treasured Early American Document**

27

*Eat their children? Eat with their children? A tiny difference, really.*

wrong." From the beginning, Sam Adams did a great job assembling pictures and words that put England in the wrong. If you really believe in something, then you want to convince lots of people that you're right. Prop-

## Tar and Feathers: Ouch!

*I thought the whole tar-and-feather thing sounded like a pretty lame punishment. So I tried it — a bad idea . . . a very bad idea.*

Sometimes all it took was a feather to send a shiver of fear down a colonial tax collector's back. If the mob caught someone they didn't like, they might strip him naked and pour hot tar all over him. Then a bushel of feathers would be dumped on the victim's head. It could take weeks to get the yucky mixture off. Often the victims were burned very badly. Their skin would come off in huge scabs, and some victims died from the burns. If the mob really wanted to make it worse, the tax collector would be ridden out of town "on a rail." Rails were logs split lengthwise into a sharp triangle, and the victim was put on the sharp side.

aganda wins people to your cause, and Sam Adams was a genius at propaganda.

One of Sam Adams's smartest acts of propaganda was to call himself and his cronies the Sons of Liberty. Some of Sam Adams's supporters in England had come up with the name. Sam sent out letters to protestors in the other colonies and told them to start calling themselves the Sons of Liberty. He helped make sure that every town had a "liberty tree." Sometimes this was a real tree; sometimes it was just a wooden pole. Sam Adams made sure everybody knew that he and his friends were dedicated to the cause of liberty. That sounded good. Doesn't Sons of Liberty sound better than a bunch of guys rioting against their mom?

## England Says "Forget Stamp Act"

Over in London, politicians realized the Stamp Act was causing more problems than it was worth. Parliament repealed it. The colonials shouted with glee! In New York, they put up a huge 15-foot gilded sculpture of George III on horseback on Bowling Green to show how grateful they were. Bowling Green was the very site of the riots against the Stamp Act. (And yes, the Dutch had bowled on this lawn. So had the English.)

## Meet the Parents

### Mercy Otis Warren (1728–1814)

Sam Adams wasn't the only propaganda genius in Massachusetts. Mercy Otis Warren used her wit to make fun of the British. She wrote plays that poked fun at them. (Making fun of your enemy is a great propaganda tool even today.) Boston was still too puritanical to put on plays, but Warren's plays were published in magazines. Her plays became popular in all 13 colonies. People loved reading them out loud to one another. Warren published anonymously because the British would have punished her or put her in jail if they'd found out who'd written the plays. Once the fighting began, Warren began a history of the American Revolutionary War; it turned into a 30-year project. After the American victory, Warren was finally able to take credit for all of her writing.

The Parliament and King George III didn't want the colonies to think mobs ruled, though. So they repealed the Stamp Act and passed a law saying they could tax the colonies whenever they wanted to. And soon they did.

The British started taxing things like paint, windowpanes, and tea. These taxes really didn't amount to much. But by now the colonies hated any taxes that went directly to England. The colonial women got their boycott going again and hit England where it hurt — in the wallet. British merchants could hardly sell a thing in America. And the whole point of having colonies was for merchants to make money. The merchants hated the uppity colonists who were stealing business from them.

In 1768, the king and Parliament sent two regiments of British infantrymen to Boston to keep order. Regiments typically were about 1,000 soldiers. The Bostonians, led by Sam Adams, refused to house British soldiers in their homes. Most of the soldiers had to pitch tents in the middle of the Boston Common.

# The Boston Massacre, or a Mob Out of Control

March 5, 1770, was a gray, cold, snow-covered day. A group of about 60 Bostonians began to taunt a British private. They claimed his commander had failed to pay for a wig. The mob grew bigger. Seven British soldiers tried to rescue the private. The mob pelted the soldiers with icy snowballs with rocks inside. A judge tried to read the Riot Act. He got so scared for his life, he ran away. The mob got bigger and more unruly. Sam Adams tried to talk them into going home. But almost nobody left.

Crispus Attucks was up on the mob's front line. More than six feet tall, Attucks was easy to spot. His mother was from the New England Natick tribe. Attucks means deer in the Natick language. His father was African. Crispus had been born a slave. He had escaped as a young

*Have you ever tried to talk to a mob? They have the worst eye contact. They're terrible listeners. And, oy! Always with the smashing and the breaking!*

man and spent much of his life at sea. Now he was one of the more than 5,200 black people living in Boston, many of them sailors.

In the mob, someone (maybe Attucks) threw a club in the air. It hit a British soldier and knocked him off his feet. The soldier got up and fired his musket. Other British soldiers panicked and began firing. Attucks was shot dead. Two boys, barely 17, were also killed. Two more people died later of gunshot wounds.

Sam Adams milked what he called the "massacre" for all it was worth. He and the other Sons of Liberty organized a funeral for Attucks and the other victims. An estimated 12,000 people marched behind the coffins. (The entire population of Boston then was only about 17,000 people.)

A few days after the massacre, Paul Revere, one of the Sons of Liberty and a master silversmith (he also made false teeth), took someone else's drawing of the massacre and turned it into an engraving. Revere sure knew how to help Sam Adams create good propaganda. His engraving showed the British soldiers lined up and deliberately firing into a peaceful crowd. Revere added bloodred touches to the picture. The engraving had nothing to do with the truth, which was that six or seven British soldiers had been surrounded by several hundred rock- and club-throwing Bostonians.

Sam Adams shipped copies of the engraving to all the other colonies and to London via the

fastest ships he could find. Just as Sam Adams had hoped, in Virginia, people like George Washington and Thomas Jefferson saw the engraving and were outraged. Maybe they didn't know anybody in Boston, but they were furious that British troops would fire on innocents. And that was exactly what Sam and John Adams wanted — for the other colonies to feel their pain.

## John Adams: Lawyer for the Defense

The morning after the Boston Massacre, John Adams was asked if he would be the lawyer who would defend the British soldiers. Some historians think that Sam Adams secretly wanted his cousin to take the job so that it wouldn't come out that the Sons of Liberty had organized the mob in the first place. But whether or not that is true, John Adams did believe in the English law that every prisoner deserved a lawyer. He took the job despite the fact that he was on the patriots' side. At the trial, Adams argued that the British soldiers had acted in self-defense because they had been threatened by the mob. The jury in Boston acquitted five of the soldiers. The two others who had actually fired their muskets were charged not with murder but with manslaughter. The soldiers were not put to death but were dishonorably discharged and branded on their thumbs.

## "Boston Harbor's a Teapot Tonight!"

After the Boston Massacre, the dispute over taxes dragged on and on. Neither side backed down. Finally, Parliament repealed the taxes, but King George felt that there must always be one tax just to make sure those cranky colonials knew that he had the right to tax them. So he and his ministers came up with a plan. The British had a lot of tea sitting around. They decided to send it to America. They would add a little tax. The tea would still be cheaper in the colonies than it was in England. The British couldn't imagine the colonists would complain! Wrong again!

On December 16, 1773, Sam Adams and the Sons of Liberty called for a mass meeting at the Old South Meeting House in Boston. More than 5,000 people showed up. The word went out.

No one should buy English tea and pay the tax, no matter how little.

Sam and his boys also had a new protest up their sleeves. They slapped on fake war paint and threw old blankets over their shoulders so they'd look like Mohawks. The British weren't fooled. They knew who it was — their enemies, the Sons of Liberty.

"Boston Harbor's a teapot tonight," cried one fake Mohawk. Silently, the men dumped 342 chests of the British tea into the water. There was no real violence. Everyone was told not to steal the tea. When one Son of Liberty was found with tea in his pockets, he was stripped naked and sent home. The vandals only broke one pad-

lock, and they even sent somebody around the next day to fix it. Nothing except the tea was touched. The tea bobbed in the water and floated away. Boys were given the job of trampling the piles of tea that washed ashore.

Sam Adams wanted to get King George's attention. He did! George III was hopping mad and so were his ministers. The colonials had gone too far by throwing their Boston Tea Party. The king was not in a partying mood. He would teach those rebels a lesson.

## You'll Pay for This!

In May 1774, King George III and his Parliament sent a fleet of warships with 3,000 British troops to Boston. The troops were under the command of General Thomas Gage, who was married to an American. The king told his troops to encircle Boston Harbor as if it were an enemy port. The people of Boston could starve until they paid for the tea. The city was closed and put under military rule. Guns were made ready to fire.

The idea that the mother country would shoot at her children and that her children would shoot back had gone from something nobody could imagine to something real . . . dangerously real.

# Ahoy,

It was such a nice day I decided to go for a sail in a sea of tea. The water here is a little bit murky, but it sure is delicious! Especially if you add a few hundred gallons of lemon juice. Mmmmmm!

I like sailing because it gets me outside and helps me forget my problems. Of course, as a roach I don't actually have any problems other than large feet and aggressive cats. I certainly have never had to pay taxes. Heck, I'd never even heard of the Stamp Act until today. One time a family I was visiting tried to squash me with their shoes and called it the Stomp Act, but that's about as close as I can get.

Speaking of getting stomped on, it sure seems like the Americans weren't going to let that happen to them, but I wonder if maybe they're biting off more than they can chew. Then again, being a roach, I always bite off more than I can chew and I'm still around. So maybe the Americans are on the right track . . . or are they???

# Chapter 2
# It's Official: We're Revolting!

A British blockade of Boston, warships in Boston's harbor— something had to be done! The radical American leaders called for a meeting of all the colonies to talk about helping Boston and bringing King George III and Parliament to their senses. The colonists decided to get together in Philadelphia, Pennsylvania. The only colony that didn't send anybody was Georgia. Georgia was kind of the baby of the colonies. It had become a colony only about 40 years earlier, and Georgia's ties to Mother England were still strong.

TIME LINE

**1774**
First Continental
Congress meets

**1775**
• April 19, Battle
  of Lexington
  and Concord,
  Massachusetts

• May 10, Second
  Continental
  Congress meets;
  Fort Ticonderoga
  taken by Ethan
  Allen and
  Benedict Arnold

# The First Continental Congress

On September 5, 1774, 56 colonial delegates assembled at Carpenter Hall in Philadelphia. Most of these guys hadn't met each other before. The delegates spent a lot of time shaking each other's hands and sizing each other up, kind of like the first day at a new school. Most of them didn't trust each other. But almost everybody was impressed with how tall and military-looking George Washington was.

A lot of the delegates didn't want a revolution. They were very suspicious of the radical Adams cousins. The delegates were certainly not ready to declare themselves independent. Instead, they sent a petition to King George asking for a repeal of all the oppressive legislation. They also passed a resolution that the colonies should arm themselves and get ready to fight if it ever proved necessary. Then they agreed to meet the following year on May 10.

On the last day of the Continental Congress, a group of delegates, including George Washington, met to say good-bye. "To His Majesty

- June 15, George Washington appointed Commander in Chief
- June 17, Battle of Bunker Hill, Massachusetts
- August 23, King George III declares a rebellion

41

## Minutemen: Ready on the Minute

All the delegates went home and told their militias to get ready to fight. All men in a community between the ages of 17 and 60 were technically in the militia, a colony's civilian army. Before 1774, most militias met just once a year. Training pretty much meant partying and drinking on the village green. Every now and then, the men would fire a musket in the air. It was kind of fun. Now, suddenly, training had to be taken seriously. Some militias began training three times a week, especially in New England. They wanted to be "ready to act at a minute warning." They became known as minutemen.

King George," they toasted. Then they lifted their glasses and said, "May the sword of the parent never be stained by the blood of his children."

## Teach 'Em a Lesson!

When King George III got the petition from the First Continental Congress, he was mad. Who were those colonists to complain that he was being unfair! He was the king! The king had men around him who told him what he wanted to hear. "They are raw undisciplined cowardly men," said British Brigadier General James Grant, who had fought with George Washington in the French and Indian War. "The Americans are hopeless soldiers, useful only as beasts of burden." The king was sure that his British soldiers could mop up those unruly kids in the blink of an eye.

The king and his ministers told General Gage to seize the rebel leaders (Sam Adams, John Hancock, and others) and grab their powder and cannons. Thanks to his spies, Gage knew that the rebels had hidden their ammunition in Concord, just a few miles outside of Boston.

## Paul Revere Goes for a Ride

Some people think Gage's beautiful American wife, Margaret Kemble Gage, spied for the rebels. The Revolution had more spies in it than you could throw a stick at. *Someone* told the Sons of Liberty that British soldiers were about to march.

> Wasn't it just a couple of pages ago that somebody threw a stick and a massacre ensued? Okay, so enough with the sticks already.

On the night of April 18, 1775, Paul Revere and William Dawes set out to warn John Hancock and Sam Adams, both of whom were staying in Lexington, near Concord. Paul Revere rode astride a very fast mare called Brown Beauty. (Okay, some historians say that nobody knows the name, but it's a nice name for a horse.) Revere and Dawes figured that even if one of them got caught, the other would get through.

Nobody yelled, "The British are coming!" Both Dawes and Revere thought of themselves as British. They shouted, "The Regulars are coming!" Both Revere and Dawes arrived in Lexington in time to warn John Hancock and Sam Adams to get out. Then they tried to go on to Concord.

Revere and Dawes rode straight into a group of redcoats on a patrol. Dawes escaped, but the

**Boston, Massachusetts.** Boston is so full of important historic places and buildings you can barely turn around without seeing one. A good bet is to follow the Freedom Trail, a two-and-a-half-mile-long redbrick line in the street. The Freedom Trail will take you to lots of Revolutionary War spots like the Old South Meeting House, the Paul Revere House, Boston Common, the Old North Church, and many others.

# Rhymin' Revere

Paul Revere was pretty much forgotten for the first hundred years after the American Revolution. Then, during the patriotic fervor of the Civil War, poet Henry Wadsworth Longfellow wrote his immortal lines:

*Listen, my children, and you shall hear*
*Of the midnight ride of Paul Revere . . .*

Some historians think Longfellow wrote about the horseback-riding silversmith because Revere rhymed with the word "hear." Poor old William Dawes was pretty much written out of history.

British soldiers held a gun to Revere's head and threatened to blow it off. Revere ended up giving them Brown Beauty or, anyway, his horse. He walked back to Concord.

## The First Shots: "Oh, What a Glorious Day"

After Paul Revere's warning, about 70 rebel minutemen gathered on Lexington Green, led by

Captain John Parker. Many were young men of 16 or 17 who were there with their fathers and grandfathers. Among them was a black man, Prince Estabrook, a slave who had volunteered to fight. The company voted to let him fight with them. (Estabrook was wounded in the battle and won his freedom as a result.)

## Warfare: A Game with Rules

In the 18th century, war was very much a game with rules. War was supposed to be glorious. Battles were often held in open fields where people could come and watch. Men wore bright, beautiful uniforms. You were not supposed to shoot at officers. Battles were fought to music, especially drumming and flute playing, which was often done by boys, some as young as 11 or 12. In the battle, the troops couldn't hear their officers so the drums were a way of barking out orders. Because the muskets couldn't fire in the rain, battles were called off if it was pouring, much like a baseball game. And battles were almost never fought in wintertime. By the rules of 18th-century warfare, if you saw you were losing a battle and were outnumbered, you were supposed to surrender gracefully. But at Lexington, the rebels started a pattern that would be repeated throughout the Revolutionary War. Instead of surrendering, they slipped back home and took their weapons with them so they could fight again.

There is still confusion about who fired the first shot on Lexington Green in the early hours of April 19, 1775. The British claimed the Americans fired first. The

Americans claimed that the British light infantry raced toward them with their bayonets fixed. However it started, soon one-ounce musket balls were flying through the air. Young Issac Muzzy died at his father's feet. Jonathan Harrington was hit in the chest. He crawled to the door of his home and died in front of his wife and son. Children and wives ran out to save their fathers and husbands. Captain Parker was wounded but kept reloading until British bayonets cut him down and killed him. When Sam Adams heard the shots, he shouted, "This is a glorious day for America!" The revolution he had longed for was beginning.

## The Americans Fight Back

In nearby Concord, the patriots had time to hide most of their gunpowder and cannons before the British fired across the North Bridge and killed two minutemen. The minutemen fired back this time, killing three British regular soldiers who died right away. Nine more British soldiers were wounded. This time it was the British who turned and ran. As word spread about the bloodshed in Lexington, thousands of militiamen from the countryside poured into the area.

Now the 700 British troops were fighting for their lives as they retreated to Boston. All along the way, American snipers fired at them from behind the cover of stone walls and trees.

The rebels kept firing their muskets; there were more and more British casualties. The march back to Boston was actually one of the bloodiest battles of the entire Revolutionary War. About 245 British soldiers were killed or wounded on the retreat. They limped back to Boston with the sounds of "Yankee Doodle Dandy" ringing in their ears.

## Two Big Egos Go for Big Guns

Now that the revolution had really started, Sam Adams knew his rebels needed cannons and ammunition. Muskets would do little good against huge cannonballs, and the British had almost all of the cannons. Willie Sutton, a famous bank robber in the 1920s, used to say that he robbed banks because that was where the money

# Who Are You Calling a Yankee Doodle Dandy?

*"Yankee Doodle came to town*
  *Riding on a pony;*
*Stuck a feather in his cap*
  *And called it Macaroni."*

"Yankee Doodle" started out as a little British ditty that made fun of the American country bumpkins. Macaroni didn't mean a noodle. Macaroni was the name for any young man who tried to put on fancy European "airs." The great thing about the song "Yankee Doodle Dandy" is that it's easy to make up new verses. The Americans soon started to make up their own verses and sang them right back at the British troops. The verse the American soldiers liked best was

*"Yankee Doodle is the tune*
*that we all delight in.*
*It suits for feasts, it suits for fun*
*and just as well for fightin'."*

was. The rebels went after British forts because that's where the cannons were. During the French and Indian War, the British had built a string of forts in the American wilderness along Lake Champlain. One of the biggest, Fort

# Don't Bother Aiming

The guns being fired by both sides were usually muskets. Muskets were big, clumsy, and hard to shoot. Each gun weighed 14 pounds and was 30 inches long. The problem was a musket couldn't be aimed. When a musket ball came out of the muzzle, it could go left, right, or center. That's why soldiers stood in a line, shoulder to shoulder. If they all fired their muskets at the same time, there was a good chance the balls would hit something.

Firing a musket took as many steps as baking a cake, sometimes more.

If everything went well, flame from the pan went through a hole into the muzzle, set fire to the gunpowder, and pushed the musket ball or bullet out. Soldiers would turn their faces away when they fired. If the fire in the pan didn't make it into the muzzle, the fire blew up in the pan and then died. "A flash in a pan" is a phrase we still use today for something that looks bright and shiny but doesn't last very long.

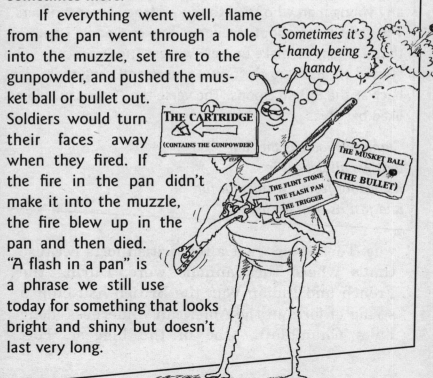

Sometimes it's handy being handy.

THE CARTRIDGE
(CONTAINS THE GUNPOWDER)

THE MUSKET BALL
(THE BULLET)

THE FLINT STONE
THE FLASH PAN
THE TRIGGER

**Minuteman National Historic Park** extends through Concord, Lincoln, and Lexington, Massachusetts. You can walk the Battle Road Trail, which takes you from Lexington to Concord on the same route the British and rebel soldiers followed during their famous battle. The trail is lined with markers describing what happened where. There are also several visitors' centers and monuments at North Bridge, the Paul Revere Capture Site, Hartwell Tavern, and Lexington Green.

Ticonderoga, also known as Fort Ti, sat on what is now the border between Vermont and New York. Two men were about to become famous by telling Sam Adams that they would take the fort.

*Anybody can go to a cannon store, but capturing a cannon is a whole different thing.*

Both Ethan Allen and Benedict Arnold knew there would be glory for the man who took Fort Ti. Benedict Arnold went north with his own troops to capture the fort. However, Ethan Allen and his Green Mountain Boys were already planning on taking it without Arnold's help. After a bunch of apparently

Loudmouth.

Troublemaker.

Oh, yeah? Well, you'll *be* forever known as the biggest traitor in American history!

**Ethan Allen**

drunken fights, Arnold and Allen agreed to attack the fort together. In the early hours of May 10, 1774, they crossed Lake Champlain and climbed the cliff to the fort together. Arnold dressed in a bright red jacket; Allen wore green. Neither let the other get ahead.

There were only 48 British soldiers in Fort Ti, most of them retired soldiers. Allen swatted one

Loudmouth.

Troublemaker.

Oh, yeah? Well, you'll *be* forever known as . . . as . . . um . . . as a furniture store!

**Benedict Arnold**

sentry with the side of his sword and forced him to take them to his leaders. A British officer came to the door in his long underwear, holding his pants. His commanding officer was still asleep. "Come out, you old rat," shouted Allen. The British saw they were outnumbered and surrendered. Not one person died. Then Ethan Allen's boys got drunk on the stores of rum in the fort and made fun of Benedict Arnold and his men for

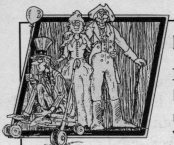

## Meet the Parents

### Ethan Allen (1738–1789)

Ethan Allen was a six-foot-four loud-mouthed giant from what is now Vermont. He loved to poke fun at the clergy. In fact, he seemed to just love trouble. He formed the Green Mountain Boys, a group of militiamen who picked fights with New Yorkers. New York at that time claimed that it owned Vermont, and so did New Hampshire. Ethan Allen often wore a green jacket that had gold shoulder pads, with an enormous sword hanging from his belt. Allen liked to swat people with the side of his sword. He actually didn't like killing.

### Benedict Arnold (1741–1801)

Benedict Arnold is famous as the number one scoundrel of the Revolutionary War. His name is still used to call someone a traitor. But at the beginning of the war, he was considered to be among the bravest and best patriot fighters. Arnold was probably at least eight inches shorter than Allen, but he was certainly his match in ego. He had a huge head and big shoulders. Some people said he looked almost deformed. Arnold was born into a wealthy family in Connecticut. However, his father was a drunk who failed in business. Arnold was elegant. He loved fancy clothes and uniforms and he was stubborn. He did what he wanted to do and asked questions later. Like Allen, he became known as a troublemaker but also as a very brave man.

being fancy dudes from Connecticut. Supposedly, some of Allen's boys even took shots at Arnold. Benedict Arnold never thought he got the credit he deserved for capturing Ticonderoga. But the important thing was that, without firing a shot, the rebels had captured 120 iron cannons, 50 swivels for guns, 16 mortars (a short gun used to fire projectiles over the walls of forts), a howitzer (another short cannon used to aim high over a fort's walls), and a warehouse full of small arms and gunpowder. The problem was that all this stuff was stuck in the Adirondack wilderness and nobody could figure out a way to move it.

## The Second Continental Congress

On the very day that Fort Ticonderoga fell, the Second Continental Congress opened in Philadelphia. They didn't know yet about Fort Ti, but the delegates were very upset about the bloodshed at Lexington and Concord. Ben Franklin had just arrived home from England. He joined the Congress. Although he, too, dreaded bloodshed, once it came, Franklin was willing to do what he could to help the fight.

As early as 1754, Franklin had suggested that the colonies form a union, much like the one that the Iroquois had. (In the Haudenosaunee League, individual Iroquois tribes kept their

**Fort Ticonderoga, New York.** This important landmark of both the French and Indian War and the Revolutionary War has been restored and rebuilt. (It's also where this author went to summer camp.) Fort Ti sits on the shore of beautiful Lake Champlain. There is a museum with lots of original military gear, and you can watch a live fife-and-drum performance or a cannon firing. You can also visit another important fort at the Crown Point State Historic Site, farther up the lake in Crown Point, New York.

You really need to stand where they tell you when they shoot the cannon.

independence but joined together for common defense.) In 1754, the British colonists refused to work together as a union. Franklin complained that the colonists had such "weak noodles" that they couldn't agree on anything. But the idea of uniting the colonies stayed with him. Now that blood had been shed, he hoped that the colonies would unite to fight the British.

Many of Franklin's fellow delegates at the Continental Congress were much more wishy-washy. They didn't see why they should risk being hanged for a bunch of radicals in Boston. However, in the meantime, they did agree that they had to send somebody up to Boston to be the commander in chief of the rabble of militias that had gathered. Eventually, this group became known as the Continental Army. But it was an army only on paper, not a real army.

The Continental Army needed a *real* general, though. The delegates couldn't help but notice that one delegate, Virginian George Washington, had shown up at the Congress in uniform. Washington wore a red-and-blue uniform he had designed himself for his militia in Virginia. All his life Washington loved uniforms. Washington claimed that he didn't want to be picked as commander in chief, he just wanted to show he was ready to fight.

Meanwhile, John Hancock felt that he was the one who should be named general. After all, Boston was his town, and he had a lot of money. John and Sam Adams didn't want Hancock. They were ever the smart politicians. They knew that in order to draw the South into their battle, they needed a southern general. On June 15, 1775, Washington was made commander in chief. John Hancock was disappointed. He never got over his jealousy of Washington.

Washington wrote to his wife, "You may believe me, my dear Patsy [George's nickname for Martha Washington], when I assure you in the most solemn manner that so far from seeking this appointment, I have used every endeavor in my power to avoid it."

## Bunker Hill, Breed Hill:
## What's the Difference?

General Washington rushed off to take over his army in Boston. Congress sent another peace petition to King George III. Peace petitions were often called olive petitions, not because the king liked olives but because an olive branch was a sign of peace.

However, before the king got the peace petition and before Washington got to Boston, a major battle took place between the rebel militias and the British. It is known as the Battle of Bunker Hill, except that most of it happened on Breed's Hill, across the Charles River in Boston.

The Americans were outnumbered and ultimately lost the battle, but the British lost more than a thousand of their men, including many of their best officers. The American dead numbered 140. In England, there was shock! These Americans rebels were not little mosquitoes that could be swatted away. General Gage wrote to London, "The rebels are not the despicable rabble too many have supposed them to be." General William Howe, an aristocrat who had won fame fighting in America in the French and Indian War, was sent to replace General Gage in Boston. Howe was considered to be a brilliant general.

# King George Declares a Rebellion

George III had had enough. When news came of Bunker Hill and the taking of Fort Ticonderoga, he had his minister declare a Proclamation of Rebellion:

*"Whereas many of my subjects in North America [have been] misled by dangerous and ill design-ing men and forgetting the allegiance which they owe . . . We have thought fit to issue our Royal Proclamation, hereby declaring that all our subjects of this realm are bound by law to be aiding and assisting in the sup-pression of such rebel-lion, and to disclose and make known all traitorous conspiracies against us.*

**A Dangerous and Ill-designed Man**

The fat was in the fire. Once the king had declared you a rebel, it was the duty of all loyal subjects to kill you or risk being killed them-selves.

# The fat was in

the fire, huh? Sounds like my kind of cookout. Speaking of food — and have you ever heard me speak about anything else? — how can our nice author Elizabeth possibly say that macaroni doesn't mean noodle?! (That's what she said. Go ahead, check it out, page 49.) She said it means when somebody is trying to act fancy or something. I know words can have different meanings sometimes, like "arms," but if macaroni's not a noodle, then how do you explain macaroni salad or macaroni and cheese?

I'm sorry to get so worked up about this, but

I need all the scraps I can get. If you take away my macaroni, next thing I know you'll be telling me that bread is just another word for money and that nut means somebody who's crazy, and . . . Hey! Wait a minute! I just lost two more of my favorite foods! I'll tell you what. Why don't we just agree that macaroni, bread, and nut can have other meanings, but the first thing we think of when we say them will always be food. Deal? Good.

Now, then, where were we? Oh, yeah! The American Revolution. I wonder how that's going.

# Chapter 3
# Do We Dare Declare?

**A**s soon as King George III had declared that the colonists were rebels, an awful lot of Americans began to have second thoughts about independence. The British offered freedom and rewards to slaves and Native Americans who revolted against the colonists. Many of the southern delegates thought to themselves, *Whoops! If we lose our slaves, we might have to work the fields ourselves... maybe we'd better make peace.* Many northerners worried about being scalped by Native Americans who sided with the British. Congress

**TIME LINE**

**1775**
Rebels fail to take Canada

**1776**
• January, Thomas Paine publishes *Common Sense*

• March 17, British evacuate Boston, Massachusetts
• July 2, Declaration of Independence

decided to send one last olive petition to the king.

Radicals, such as Sam Adams and John Adams, worried that they'd never get the colonies to declare independence. Sam Adams wrote that some of the members of Congress had the "vanity of the ape, the tameness of the ox, or the stupid servility of the ass." Even John Hancock changed his mind about declaring independence. He was still angry with both Adamses for picking Washington, not him, to lead the army.

**Little Johnny Hancock Gets an Idea**

## Is This Any Way to Run an Army?

Meanwhile, outside of Boston, George Washington was having a tough time. There were almost 3,000 colonial troops gathered around Boston. The rebel army camp in Cambridge, right outside Boston, was a rowdy, undisciplined tent city. The outhouses were stinking messes and cesspools. Most of the soldiers didn't have uniforms. Many didn't have muskets; some just had

pitchforks and sickles. Many men brought their families with them. The women and children cooked, cleaned, and helped make cartridges.

Washington was a rather spit-and-polish kind of military man, and this wasn't his idea of a real army. It certainly wasn't one big, happy family. The New Jersey volunteers didn't want to take orders from the Connecticut volunteers. The New England volunteers didn't want to take orders from anyone. There were constant fights between different companies, particularly if they were from different colonies. And then in the middle of this mix, Dan Morgan brought up some sharpshooters from the backcountry of Virginia. They didn't like anybody, and nobody liked them.

## George Washington Throws a Temper Tantrum

One day, Dan Morgan's gang from Virginia got into a snowball fight with men from the

## Dan Morgan Takes a Lickin' and Keeps on Tickin'

Dan Morgan was one soldier who had plenty of reason to hate the British. During the French and Indian War, he got into a fight with a British officer and was sentenced to 500 lashes with a whip. Most men would have died, but not Dan Morgan. He lived to laugh about it, even saying they had missed one lash because the drummer boy had miscounted. Morgan was six feet tall and weighed about 200 pounds. The British would come to wish that he had died, because he was one of the best shots in the army. Daniel Morgan used a rifle. Unlike muskets, rifles had a bore in the muzzle that made the bullet come out in a straight line. But rifles were harder to load than muskets, and you couldn't fit a bayonet on a rifle, so most soldiers didn't use them. Unfortunately for the British, Dan Morgan did. He could hit a target the size of a man's head from 150 yards with a rifle — something unheard of with a musket.

Marblehead, Massachusetts, regiment. Soon 1,000 soldiers were punching and kicking one another in the slush.

When General Washington heard about the fight, he leaped on his horse, soared over a fence, and landed in the middle of the brawl. He grabbed two soldiers by their shirts, lifted them off the ground, and knocked their heads together.

"From the moment I saw Washington leap the bars at Cambridge, I never faltered in the faith that we had the right man to lead the cause of American liberty," wrote Major General John Sullivan from New Hampshire.

## Oh, Canada! Want to Be the 14th State?

Sam Adams thought he had a plan that would bring a quick victory. Take Canada! Adams was sure that Canada was ripe to join the rebellion. All the Canadians needed was a little push. Guess which two men were ready and willing to do the pushing? Ethan Allen and Benedict Arnold! But Congress gave command of the invasion of Canada to neither Allen nor Arnold. Aristocratic New Yorker Philip Schuyler got the job. Schuyler was an awful general. He was

From the general, sir. He can't come to the war today. This is a note from his mom.

always sick and could never make up his mind. Finally, he turned over his command to Richard Montgomery. Washington, who liked Benedict Arnold, told him that he could invade Canada at the head of his own little army of 1,100 by going through Maine. Daniel Morgan volunteered to go with Arnold.

In September 1775, Arnold and Morgan started their march to Canada. The trip was a nightmare. The rivers were full of torrential waterfalls. The men nearly died as they waded through freezing water. They ran out of food. They ate soap. They boiled

*When Washington's army was forced to eat its shoes, Private Jingles was no longer an object of ridicule.*

their leather moccasins into soup. A lot of the soldiers deserted and just went home.

They finally reached Quebec in December, where they joined Montgomery. On New Year's Eve, December 31, 1775, the Americans attacked in a howling blizzard. The Canadians in the city of Quebec did not want to join the rebels. They fought back. The invasion of Canada was a disaster for the Americans. Montgomery was killed; Benedict Arnold was wounded. Even Dan Morgan was captured, although he fought like a hellcat until the end. Of the 1,650 men who invaded Canada, 100 were dead or wounded, 300 were captured. The remaining men just wanted to go home.

## George Washington Gets Some Guns

While some rebel troops were attacking Canada, the bulk of the rebel army was with Washington in Cambridge. Morale was low. Most men had only enlisted for six months or a year. Washington knew he needed a steady army of at least 20,000 to beat the British. By January 1, 1776, he was left with just 5,582 soldiers to ring the forts that had been built. The crisis changed Washington's mind about enlisting African Americans in the Continental Army. When he'd taken over in July, he had been afraid that most southerners wouldn't fight side by side with African Americans, so he had told his men not to let them reenlist. But now that he really needed them, Washington wrote to Congress that the African Americans who were serving with him should be allowed to stay, and Congress voted to allow them to reenlist.

Washington didn't just lack men. He also lacked guns and cannons. He had no artillery to speak of. (Artillery means all the big weapons like cannons that can be moved around to attack the enemy's positions.) All those cannons that

Benedict Arnold and Ethan Allen had captured in Fort Ticonderoga more than six months before were still sitting 300 miles and several mountain gaps away. Washington was desperate for them. Luckily, help was on the way from a very unexpected source.

## Meet the Parents

### Henry Knox (1750–1806)

Henry Knox was a fat young bookseller from Boston. As a teenager, he'd shot off the third and fourth fingers of one hand in a hunting accident. But Henry Knox loved guns and loved to study war and ancient battles. In any other time, he probably would have lived out his life in his bookstore, moving around toy soldiers and cannons. But Henry Knox lived in interesting times, and he took advantage of them. At almost every important point of the Revolution, Henry Knox was there. He became one of Washington's most loyal aides. Knox was never skinny, even during the starving times of the Revolution. After the war, he weighed about 300 pounds. When Washington became President, Henry Knox was made the new country's first Secretary of War. (Today, the cabinet post is called Secretary of the Defense.) Knox died at age 56 when a chicken bone got caught in his intestines.

# Henry Knox Gets an Ox

Even though Henry Knox was only 25, Washington put him in charge of all the placement of the artillery. This was and still is one of the most important tactical jobs in a war. Knox told General Washington he'd bring him the cannons from Fort Ti. And by George, he did it. In the middle of winter, Knox used huge oxen and big horses to pull sleds mounted with 59 artillery pieces weighing 120,000 pounds. It was a trip of more than 300 miles. Along with all the cannons, Knox also brought Washington about 2,300 pounds of lead to be melted down into bullets. Washington was so happy, he could have hugged Henry Knox if he had been the hugging kind of general. Instead, Washington promoted him and kept Knox close to his side for the rest of the war.

# The British Leave Boston

In March 1776, Washington lined up his cannons in Dorchester, in the hills surrounding Boston. When British General Howe saw these cannons, he said in astonishment, "My god! These fellows have done more work in one night than I could have made my army do in three months."

Bottled up in Boston Harbor, Howe bombarded the American cannons from his warships while he figured out what to do. The king's ministers wanted him to take New York City. They had studied maps of the colonies and decided that New York was the key, not Boston. Howe decided to abandon Boston.

On the morning of March 17, 11,000 British soldiers and sailors and perhaps 1,000 colonial loyalists boarded ships and sailed away from Boston, but not before blowing up the main British headquarters and looting the city. Washington watched them go through his spyglass. He was amazed, but he knew the war wasn't over. Washington could read maps as well as the British. He knew the British would try to take New York. He marched his army south.

# New York, New York:
# It's a Loyalist Town

On April 13, 1776, Washington arrived in New York City before the British. He and Henry Knox examined the city to see how they could defend it. They realized right away that New York would be far harder to defend than Boston. It was surrounded by water, and the British had the greatest navy in the world. The rebels had no navy. Even worse, New York was full of people who were loyal to the king. A lot of New Yorkers thought the rebels were a bunch of dirty, crazy people who only wanted to make trouble. There were even plots to kill Washington by feeding him poisoned peas or stabbing him in the back.

# Knocking Some Common Sense into Congress

While General Washington was in New York trying to figure out how to defend it, Congress was still stuck in Philadelphia. The awful news of the defeat in Canada reached them. Many of the delegates were willing to throw in the towel, surrender, and beg the king for mercy.

At that crucial point, while the politicians were waffling, a little pamphlet was published that set America on fire. Written by Thomas Paine, *Common Sense* outlined the reasons for

# Meet the Parents

## Alexander Hamilton (1757–1804)

No New Yorker was more loyal to General Washington than young Alexander Hamilton. He was born in the West Indies, and his mother never married his father. As an orphaned teenager, Hamilton came to New York City without much money. He joined the rebellion because he wanted a world where it didn't matter who you were born to. If you had enough pluck and luck to make money, you could rise. The American Revolution gave him his chance.

Hamilton stood five-foot-seven, had red hair and high cheekbones, and the ladies loved him. They said he didn't need any "sand in his stockings." In those days, men wore tight stockings and breeches. Some men would put sand "falsies" in their stockings when they went dancing to make their calves look more muscular. On the battlefield and for causes he believed in he could fight like a tiger. His high passions made him plenty of enemies.

*As with all fads, there are always those who take things way too far.*

independence in simple words that anybody could understand. In less than three months, more than 120,000 copies of *Common Sense* were sold, which would equal 15 million books today.

## Congress Stiffens Its Spine

The popularity of *Common Sense* helped push Congress toward independence. Then Washington's spies found out that King George III had signed treaties with different groups of German princes to hire 18,000 of their troops to fight against the Americans. The German troops were often called "Hessians" after one of the German principalities. The idea that their British king would pay foreign soldiers to kill them shocked most Americans and pushed the people toward independence.

Before Congress could declare independence, it had to set up a committee. Congresses always love committees. It picked a committee to write a "Declaration of Independence." Ben Franklin and John Adams were both on the committee,

# Meet the Parents

## Thomas Paine (1737–1809)

In England, Thomas Paine had been a corset maker. (Corsets were the combination brassieres and waist-cinchers that women wore. They were very uncomfortable.) He'd failed at making corsets. He'd failed at running a grocery store and being a teacher. He'd even failed in his two marriages. In 1774, Paine came to America. He wrote essays attacking slavery and also wrote that it was wrong to treat women as if they didn't have any rights. Then he wrote *Common Sense,* his essay on why the colonies should be independent, and his words changed history: *"Mother Nature hates kings or she wouldn't have put so many asses on the throne. . . . Oh ye! that love mankind! Ye that dare oppose not only the tyranny but the tyrant, stand forth! Every spot of the old world is overrun with oppression. Freedom hath been hunted round the globe. O! receive the fugitive, and prepare in time an asylum for mankind."*

Hey, what do you call it when you fail at making corsets, selling groceries, and teaching? "Paineful!" Get it? "Painful!" That's a pun. I'm being punny. Get it? Punny? Is this thing on?

# Meet the Parents

## Thomas Jefferson (1743–1826)

Born on one of his father's tobacco plantations in Virginia, Thomas Jefferson was only 14 when his father died and left him everything. At 15, Jefferson was among the richest men in the colonies and owner of more than 200 slaves. He was very tall, nearly six-foot-four, sandy-haired, and he freckled easily. Jefferson was almost as good a horseback rider as Washington, and he loved hunting but not as much as his music and books. Jefferson went to law school and, like most well-educated men of his standing, entered politics. He hated making speeches, but very early on his friends and peers realized that he was a very good writer. In an age when most politicians spent their times in taverns, Jefferson much preferred his books, music, writing, and conversation with just a few people. He played the violin several hours a day. He liked inventing things almost as much as Franklin did, especially practical things, but Jefferson was anything but practical. He was an architect whom some consider one of the best of all time, but he never finished his own home. He invented a bed that could disappear into a wall and a little writing desk that was the size of a book. He brought the portable writing desk with him to Philadelphia. William Shakespeare once said that words and poetry last far longer than any palaces or statues. The words that Jefferson wrote on that tiny portable desk have proved to be immortal.

but John Adams wanted to make sure that the southern colonies felt they were important. Virginia was the most populous southern colony, so he suggested a Virginia delegate, Thomas Jefferson, for the committee. At 32, Jefferson was one of the youngest men in Congress.

Jefferson wrote the Declaration of Independence during a heat wave at the end of June 1776. His room in Philadelphia was so hot and stuffy that he could only write late at night and in the early morning, after soaking his feet in a basin of cold water to cool off. Jefferson wrote the first draft in just two days. Ever since he had been a student, he'd had one rule that all writers should follow: "Never use two words when one will do." With his quill pen, Jefferson wrote and rewrote, scratching out words and phrases. He took what he had written to Adams and Franklin, who suggested some changes. But Jefferson's first words remained pretty much untouched. Those words changed the world forever.

LOOK!

. . . out? Hmmm. I guess "Never use two words when one will do" isn't always the best rule.

## Jefferson Tries to End the Slave Trade

Jefferson listed all the reasons why the colonies felt King George had mistreated them and why they must be free. He wrote a long passage in his original draft that called for the end of the slave trade and condemned King George for allowing it. But many southerners and New Englanders had grown rich because of the slave trade. They refused to sign the Declaration if it included Jefferson's tough antislavery language. How could Jefferson say that all men are created equal and still own slaves? He knew he couldn't, and he struggled with the issue of slavery all his life.

## The First July 4 Was on July 2

On July 1, 1776, Congress began its final debate on independence. The temperature soared into the 90s. When it was John Adams's turn to speak, the skies opened up with thunder and lightning and pouring rain. It became so dark that candles had to be lit. Adams spoke louder so he could be heard against the crashing thunder as he helped convince most of the timid members that the time had come.

The next day, July 2, 1776, Congress finally voted for independence. John Adams wrote that the "second day of July ought to be celebrated with pomp and parade, with shows, games, guns, sports,

# Announcing the Birth of a New Nation

*We hold these Truths to be self-evident, that all Men are created equal, that they are endowed, by their CREATOR, with certain unalienable Rights, that among these are Life, Liberty, and the Pursuit of Happiness. . . . We, therefore, the Representatives of the united States of America . . . declare that these united Colonies are, and of Right ought to be Free and Independent States . . .*

This was the first time that the words *the United States of America* had ever been used in an official document.

bells, bonfires, and illuminations [fireworks]."

On July 4, the final draft of the Declaration was approved. That's the day that's been celebrated as Independence Day ever since. John

# Remember the Ladies

John Adams had been on the committee to write the Declaration of Independence, and as usual he and his wife, Abigail, had exchanged letters about it. Abigail warned him, *"Remember the Ladies . . . and be more generous and favorable to them than your ancestors . . . Remember all Men would be tyrants if they could. If particular care and attention is not paid to the Ladies we are determined to foment a Rebellion and will not hold ourselves bound by any Laws in which we have no voice or Representation."* John wrote back to her. *"I cannot but laugh . . . you are so saucy."* As John Adams's reply suggests, he didn't take women's rights seriously. Except for Tom Paine, who advocated women's rights, John Adams and the others did nothing for women. But when New Jersey wrote its new state constitution on July 2, 1776, it accidentally gave women the right to vote, and they kept it until 1807 when it was repealed.

*Go ahead, John Adams. Don't listen to me, dearest friend. Don't give women the vote. Our little John Quincy Adams here is going to grow up to be President someday. He'll give his mommy the vote, won't you, honey?*

*How long till they invent Gameboy?*

Hancock was the first one to sign it. He made his signature huge, saying, "so the king doesn't have to put on his glasses [to read it]." Even today, if you're asked to put your John Hancock on something, it means to sign your name. "There must be no pulling different ways," said Hancock as he put down his signature.

"Yes," Benjamin Franklin replied. "We must all hang together. Or most assuredly we shall all hang separately."

## Phillis Wheatley (c. 1753–1784)

Phillis Wheatley was born in Africa, kidnapped, and sold at a slave auction at about age seven to a rich Boston family named Wheatley. She learned to read along with the Wheatley children. Wheatley learned Greek and Latin on her own. She loved the great English poets and began to write her own poetry. Many white people couldn't believe that an African woman had written those poems herself.

When Boston turned into a hotbed of revolutionary fervor, Phillis Wheatley helped the cause by writing poems about the Boston Massacre and the revolutionary leaders. She even got to meet George Washington, who admired her poetry. In 1773, the Wheatleys freed Phillis. She married John Peters, a free black man, in 1778.

# Happy Fourth

of July, everybody!! I know it may not actually be the Fourth of July, but I feel like celebrating, anyway. I learned two very interesting things today. One, that Thomas Jefferson was the first person to ever write down the name united States of America, and two, if I put sand in my stockings the ladies will love me. (I've always had sort of spindly legs. Think I'll go get a pail and shovel.)

Now, then, I don't know about you, but I'm starting to feel prouder to be an American with every page I turn. All these people were so much braver than I am. The only one I had anything in common with was the guy who died after he swallowed a chicken bone. Knox, I think his name was. It's a silly way to die, but like my grandpa always used to tell me, "If you gotta go, you may as well go eating chicken." Come to think of it, I never knew what the heck he was talking about until now. Maybe I didn't give my grandpa as much credit as he deserved.

Anyway, now that the states of America are united, I bet all their problems are behind them. Of course, I've been wrong before. . . .

# Chapter 4
# You Can Win by Losing

**A**fter the Declaration of Independence, Congress immediately began arguing about how to run things. They eventually wrote something they called the Articles of Confederation. Under the Articles, each state had one vote. The Articles couldn't be changed unless all the states agreed. According to the Articles, Congress didn't have any authority to raise taxes on its own. They had to ask the states for money; many states just said no.

TIME LINE

**1776**
• August, Washington loses Battle of Brooklyn and New York
•September, Washington loses New York City; Nathan Hale hanged; Franklin sent to France

• November, Washington retreats through New Jersey
• December, Tom Paine writes *The Crisis*; Battle of Trenton, New Jersey

**1777**
Washington headquarters in Morristown, New Jersey

84

Meanwhile, General Washington was left with little or no money to pay his troops. British spies were happy to report that the Americans couldn't agree on much of anything and that Washington's army, waiting for them in New York, was miserable. Britain was ready to get serious.

## The Mighty British Sail into New York

On the morning of June 29, 1776, New Yorkers woke up and found that that the entire harbor was full of British ships. During the night, General Howe had arrived with more than 30,000 troops and hundreds of ships to take New York City. It was the largest movement of an army and navy in the world since ancient times.

Just at that moment, Washington got a copy of the Declaration of Independence. Washington was filled with sadness that this final step had finally been taken, but he hoped it would inspire his men. He had the Declaration read out loud to his troops and to a large group of civilians. A cheering mob marched down Broadway to

Bowling Green and pulled down the gilded statue of King George III. It was melted down to make 42,088 lead musket balls.

However, most New Yorkers, when they saw the size of the navy and troops lined up against them, decided to remain loyal to the king. It seemed to most of them that the rebels would be squashed like bugs. Washington had no navy to use to fight. There was nothing the Continental Army could do to stop the British ships from firing on the city with their big guns.

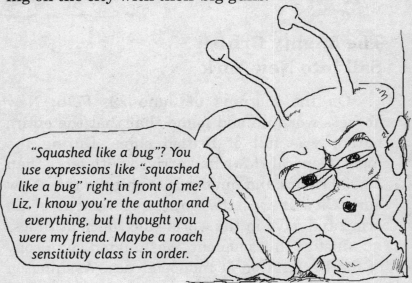

"Squashed like a bug"? You use expressions like "squashed like a bug" right in front of me? Liz, I know you're the author and everything, but I thought you were my friend. Maybe a roach sensitivity class is in order.

## The Battle of Brooklyn

Brooklyn is one of the biggest parts of New York City. One of the most important battles of the Revolutionary War was fought there. Yet more people know about Lexington and Concord than know about the Battle of Brooklyn. Maybe it's because the Americans lost big-time. (The Battle of Brooklyn is sometimes called the Battle of Long Island, but this New Yorker and most historians prefer to call it the Battle of Brooklyn.)

Washington tried to stop the British from invading New York by throwing his entire army of about 13,000 men at them in Brooklyn. The Battle of Brooklyn was the first time Washington's army faced well-trained British and German troops in the open field. And they got whomped. The 22,000 disciplined British and German soldiers overwhelmed Washington's troops. Loyalists in Brooklyn led the British

## Well, We Did Have a Turtle

The rebels didn't have a navy, but David Bushnell, a young graduate of Yale, and his brother invented a one-person submarine. He called it the "turtle," and it operated by foot pedals. Bushnell got someone to try it out in New York harbor. The plan was to place an explosive mine on the British warship the HMS *Eagle*. It didn't work. The mine wouldn't stick to the ship and the turtle had to skedaddle out of there. Eventually, the British got tired of people trying to blow them up from underwater, and they began sinking anything that came near them, including the turtle.

troops around the American troops so that they could be attacked from behind.

Trapped and panicked, the Americans either surrendered or fled into the woods. They were hunted down like animals. The Hessian troops bayoneted the Americans even as they tried to surrender. The Germans had been told that the American rebels would do the same to them. So they killed first.

## Washington Rows Away

After the first day of the Battle of Brooklyn, Washington had 9,000 troops still alive. They were trapped in Brooklyn, their backs to the water. If Washington let them be captured, the rebellion

## Prison Ships, a Slow Way to Die

The rebel soldiers who did survive after they surrendered were put onto rotting prison ships in New York
Harbor. Over the course of the war, more than 11,500 men
died aboard these death traps. In the middle of the war,
Elizabeth Burgin of New York City helped arrange the
escape of more than 200 prisoners. She had a price put on
her head, and Washington helped arrange her escape on a
whaleboat to Philadelphia.

would be over. Washington took 18th-century rules
of conduct seriously. He considered himself an officer and a gentleman, and he knew that if you lost
a battle, you were supposed to lay down your
arms. The proper thing to do was to surrender.

But Washington also knew that if he surrendered his army, there would be no independence, no United States of America. He decided
to forget about what was proper; he would do
what was necessary to stay alive.

On August 29, Washington rushed orders
across the river to Manhattan to collect every
boat, especially flat-bottomed rowboats that could
hold heavy loads and horses. He had just a few
hours of darkness to try to sneak his troops across
the East River under the noses of the British.

Washington didn't even tell his own troops they were running away. He told them to join him down at the river to meet new recruits from New Jersey. When the troops got down to the river's edge, they were told to silently march onto little boats, carrying their guns and leading their horses. A few boatloads at a time, an entire army crossed over to Manhattan. The last man on the last boat was George Washington. The British

All right, Washington, give yourself up. I'm not going to ask again. I'm not kidding! Okay, I'm counting to three. . . .

ferried themselves across and gave chase, but by then the Americans had a head start.

Once in Manhattan, General Washington and his men retreated up Broadway. Now, his troops were in complete panic. It was the opposite of an orderly retreat. Watching it all from his horse, Washington yelled, "Are these the men with whom I am to defend America?" He used his

**TRAVEL**

**Brooklyn, New York.** Some years there is a live reenactment of the Battle of Brooklyn in Prospect Park, a huge, beautiful park in the middle of Brooklyn. You can watch the battle and see all sorts of demonstrations of what life and warfare in the 18th century were like. You can visit the Old Stone House a few blocks away, where the Americans bravely tried to hold off the British. There's also a memorial to the Marquis de Lafayette in the park, at the corner of Ninth Street and Prospect Park West, and a memorial to those prisoners of war in Fort Greene Park, Brooklyn.

riding crop and whipped the soldiers who were running away. Never again, until the end of the war, would Washington commit his entire army to a battle.

Somewhere around where Manhattan's 42nd Street is today, Washington just gave up. He sat slumped on his horse and stared into space. Hessian soldiers were just 80 yards away. They recognized the American general and could have shot him, but they thought it was a trap. Finally, an aide found Washington and led him away by his horse's reins. Washington retreated north to Harlem Heights near where 125th Street is now.

# Patriotic Nathan Hale, Not a Very Good Spy

Stuck up in Harlem, General Washington needed spies to go back down to New York City and find out what the enemy was up to. Nathan Hale, a schoolteacher just 21 years old, volunteered to go. Nathan Hale was not a very good spy. He wrote notes to himself that weren't in code, and he kept the notes in his coat pocket. He lasted only two weeks. His loyalist cousin, Samuel Hale, might have betrayed him. Nathan Hale was captured. He was out of uniform and had the incriminating documents on him. Near where 42nd Street is today, the British hanged him without a trial. He was asked if he had any last words to say, and his last words made him famous: "I only regret that I have but one life to lose for my country." Then he was hanged by the neck until he died.

**When You're a Bad Plumber**

**When You're a Bad Cook**

**When You're a Bad Kid**

**When You're a Bad Spy**

The retreat from New York was bloody. While General Howe was suspected of having sympathetic feelings toward the Americans, his second in command, General Lord Charles Cornwallis, was a brilliant general who had no qualms about squashing the rebels. Cornwallis felt the quicker it could be done, the better. He chased the remnants of Washington's troops ruthlessly. The rebel troops took refuge in forts near the tip of Manhattan. At Fort Washington, they were short of troops. Margaret Corbin's husband was killed beside his cannon. Margaret took his place and was hit by three bullets. After the battle, a medic walking among the dead and wounded saw her hand move. He sent her in a wagon to Philadelphia, her left arm nearly torn from her body. Corbin was permanently disabled, with her face and arm badly scarred. In July 1777, she was made part of the Invalid Regiment, soldiers who had been disabled fighting in the war. In 1779, she became the first woman to receive a military pension.

## New Jersey: More Bloodshed There Than Any Other State

In many towns in New Jersey, you can see signs that say GEORGE WASHINGTON SLEPT HERE! Well, most of those signs are true. Washington moved all over New Jersey to keep his army alive while Lord Cornwallis and the British were chasing him.

Washington had to keep his soldiers moving. The rebels were exhausted. They marched at night, and they never rested anywhere comfortable for long. They were literally on the run; in fact, one-fifth of them had dysentery, which is a fancy name for diarrhea or the "runs."

Those guys would've loved one of these! Perfect for the soldier "on the run"!

In November 1776, the British offered the rebels a chance to surrender with honor. They offered all rebels in New Jersey a royal pardon. In just two weeks, 3,000 accepted, including one signer of the Declaration. By December 1776, all of New Jersey was in the hands of the British. Washington and his troops fled across the Delaware River into Pennsylvania farmland. Cornwallis's 10,000 troops waited for the river to freeze so they could cross over and finish off the

Continental Army. Washington knew he was done for. "I think the game is pretty near up," he wrote his brother. British troops were just 30 miles from Philadelphia. Congress fled to Baltimore.

## The British Take a Break . . . and Give Washington a Break

Right about then, the British General Howe declared the war over for the winter. Remember: in the 18th century, it was common to stop wars in winter. General Howe settled in New York City. He and his British officers entertained at balls and banquets and theatrical events. Cornwallis's troops were ordered to winter in New Jersey. Some Hessian troops settled in Trenton, right across the Delaware River from Washington's troops.

The winter of 1776 was bitterly cold. Washington's army was down to just 6,000 men. His soldiers had no tents and little winter clothing. It was just before Christmas. Like the previous year, most of the men's enlistments were up on December 31. In one week, General Washington knew he'd have almost no army. Washington was very frustrated. He wrote to his cousin, "If I were to wish the bitterest curse to a worst enemy . . . I should put him in my stead . . . I do not know what plan of conduct to pursue . . . I am wearied to death."

## Victory or Death

In December 1776, Hessian troops fighting for the British were getting ready to celebrate Christmas in Trenton. Washington desperately needed a victory to prove to Congress and to the people that the cause wasn't lost. So once again, he decided to move horses and cannons across a river in the middle of the night.

On December 25, Washington ordered his men to learn the password "victory or death." They were not to let anyone near them who didn't know the password in case loyalist spies were lurking in the countryside. The soldiers were rowed across the Delaware River on boats that were like long canoes, 60 feet long but only six feet wide. Their

# These Are the Times
# That Try Men's Souls

When things were bleakest in December 1776, Tom Paine, who had enlisted in the army as a private, sat down by an army campfire and wrote on a drumhead: *"These are the Times that try men's souls. The summer soldier and the sunshine patriot will, in this crisis, shrink from the service of his country; but he that stands it now, deserves the love and thanks of man and woman. Tyranny, like Hell, is not easily conquered; yet . . . the harder the conflict, the more glorious the triumph."* His words were published in another little pamphlet called *The American Crisis*. Once again Paine's writing changed history. Washington had *The Crisis* read aloud to his troops. Many men agreed to stay with Washington. Paine's words were as inspiring then as they are now.

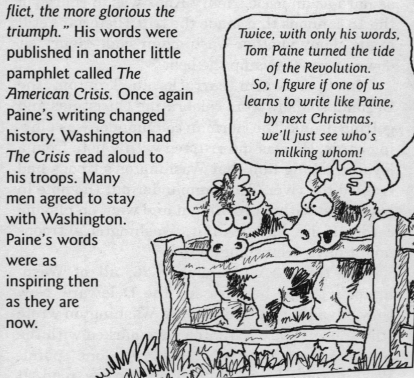

*Twice, with only his words, Tom Paine turned the tide of the Revolution. So, I figure if one of us learns to write like Paine, by next Christmas, we'll just see who's milking whom!*

horses panicked with the rocking of the boats, and every piece of clothing that was splashed turned as hard as an icicle. Henry Knox was in charge of the 18 cannons that made the trip. Historians still argue about whether Washington said, "Henry, sit down or you'll swamp the boat."

In their warm barracks in Trenton, the German soldiers were celebrating Christmas and getting drunk. The German commander was playing cards. He was interrupted with a note from a loyalist telling him that Washington's troops had crossed the river. The commander put the note in his pocket without reading it and went on playing cards. If he had read it, Washington's troops might have been slaughtered.

By three A.M. December 26, all of Washington's troops had crossed the Delaware. Now they advanced on their enemy. Washington wrote "the snowy road to Trenton was marked with the blood of my soldiers' feet." At one point, Washington's horse slipped on the icy road. It looked as if he and his steed were going to crash down an icy bank. Washington steadied the horse with one of his big hands on the horse's mane. Pulling on the reins, he heaved the horse back to safety. "I knew then," wrote one of his men, "that we would not lose." Wrapped in a cloak, Washington whispered to his men to have courage and to stick by their officers.

Early in the morning, Washington's troops appeared out of the sleet and snow and attacked! The Hessian regiment was drunk and asleep. The Germans soldiers tried to form lines in their underwear, shouting *"Der Feind! Heraus! Heraus!"* (The enemy! Get up! Get up!)

The Hessians were surrounded. One hundred and six of them were killed or wounded. More than 900 officers and soldiers surrendered. Some reports said not one American died. Others reported that two were killed in action, and two or three froze to death. Finally, Washington had proved that his Continental Army could actually win a fight.

Flag on the play! Illegal use of troops during winter break. Penalty goes to . . . um . . . how about "to the victors go the spoils"?

# Washington Refuses to Be a Dictator

Congress was so happy that Washington had actually won a battle that on the last day of the year, December 31, 1776, they gave Washington powers that would have made him a dictator. They told him he had the power to take any supplies he needed if loyalists wouldn't sell them and to arrest anybody who was disloyal to the "American cause." Washington refused. "The sword was the last resort for the preservation of our liberties, so it ought to be the first thing laid aside when those liberties are firmly established." He refused to force loyalists or people who were neutral to take continental money when they were afraid it was worth nothing. Many historians believe that of the many great moments of Washington's life, this was one of the greatest.

Washington didn't have any way to take care of the prisoners of war. He treated his German prisoners much better than his men had been treated in Brooklyn. He took their arms away and offered the Germans the chance to stay in America. Many took him up on that offer and later became farmers.

## Hey, France!
## Are You Impressed Yet?

The American rebels were counting on the old saying that "the enemy of my enemy is my friend." When the nations in Europe heard that

Washington had actually won a couple of battles, France and Spain began to think that maybe these Americans were more than "a flash in the pan."

France and Spain began secretly funneling money and aid to the rebels, but they wanted to wait and see before they jumped into the war. However, even though the French king, Louis XVI, refused to enter the war openly, many of his countrymen were inspired by the fight for liberty and decided to go to America on their own.

## French Go Wild for Franklin

In the late fall of 1776, after helping write the Declaration of Independence, Ben Franklin got a new title, United States minister to France. It was one of the most important jobs in the new country because without France's help, everyone knew the Revolution would fail. Franklin was perfect for France. He was already famous as a scientist and a philosopher. He was a walking advertisement for America. Paris loved him, and he loved Paris. Court ladies fought for the chance to sit on his lap. Talk about propaganda! Franklin even started wearing a coonskin cap instead of a powdered wig to advertise that he was the symbol of the New America. He became France's favorite person. Franklin's portrait was painted countless times. His picture appeared on beer glasses, on china, and even on chamber pots, the pots that people peed in before there were indoor toilets.

However popular Franklin was, French King Louis XVI would not see him at court. The king wanted proof that the Americans could win a major battle. The American rebels were going to have to do better than capture a bunch of Hessians before the French court officially entered the war.

# Meet the Parents

## Marquis de Lafayette (1757–1834)

The Marquis de Lafayette was a French aristocrat who was one of the wealthiest men in the world. Think of modern billionaires and you'd have Lafayette. As a teenager, he'd decided that the fight for freedom in America was where he must go for glory. Lafayette was almost 20 and didn't have much experience. He wanted to be a major general. Lafayette was so eager to help that Washington couldn't bear to turn him away. He gave him a position at his headquarters, and Lafayette more than proved his faith in him. Soon, he became one of the most trusted young men at Washington's headquarters. Lafayette used his own money to buy his men blankets, food, and supplies. He spent an estimated $200,000 during the American Revolution (worth many a million today).

### An Amended Old Riddle

*What do a 500-pound gorilla and a 19-year-old millionaire do?*

*Anything they want!*

# Well, here I am,

crossing the Delaware River with General George Washington, and I, like Nathan Hale, have but one regret — that I didn't bring a heavy jacket! It's freezing out here! Now I understand why the British didn't like to fight in the winter. Whoever said "war is hell" had no idea how cold it gets in New Jersey in the middle of December. Maybe if I try really hard I can sit back and pretend I'm actually enjoying a nice, warm cup of tea while seven of my closest friends crawl in and out of a delicious, day-old crumpet. Now that's living!

But I guess you can't win a war if you just keep running away. Anyway, you heard what the British said about the rebel troops, that they would "squash us like bugs." Who do they think they are, saying something like that?!

Those are fightin' words! And fight I will!!! But first things first, I've got to get a heavy jacket. Seriously, it's freezing out here.

# Chapter 5
# Stalemate

**T**he Revolutionary War bogged down for quite a while. The British troops controlled New York and New Jersey. But George Washington had kept his army alive.

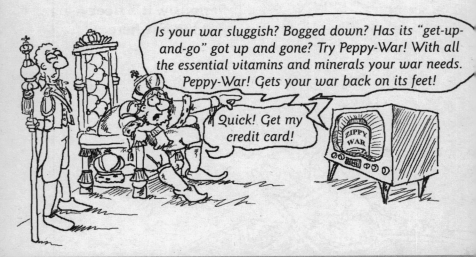

Is your war sluggish? Bogged down? Has its "get-up-and-go" got up and gone? Try Peppy-War! With all the essential vitamins and minerals your war needs. Peppy-War! Gets your war back on its feet!

Quick! Get my credit card!

ZIPPY WAR

TIME LINE

**1777**
• July, British take back Fort Ticonderoga

• September, British chase Congress out of Philadelphia, Pennsylvania

• October, British General Burgoyne defeated at Saratoga, New York

106

## Meet Gentleman Johnny

King George III told General Burgoyne, nick-named Gentleman Johnny, to put an end to the stalemate. The king gave the general a huge army of almost 8,000 soldiers, half of them Hessians. Burgoyne's mission? Attack the rebels from Canada. At the same time, General Howe was supposed to attack from New York. All those nasty rebels in New England would be squeezed like a gerbil in the coils of a boa constrictor.

Burgoyne was an aristocratic, charming gambler. He said he'd mop up the rebel operation in a few months.

## Iroquois Fight for the British

Gentleman Johnny recruited almost 4,000 Iroquois to serve as his scouts. The Iroquois, still the largest Native American alliance in the Northeast, thought fighting for the British was the lesser of two evils. The Iroquois didn't love the British, but the British treated them much better than the colonists did.

| 1777–78 | 1778 | 1779–80 |
|---|---|---|
| Washington's army stuck in Valley Forge, Pennsylvania | France comes into the war | Benedict Arnold turns traitor |

Sir, our guides have abandoned us. We're lost and the enemy is closing in on us. And we're out of champagne.

CHAMPAGNE!!!! We're out of champagne???!!!!

On July 1, 1777, Burgoyne and his Iroquois allies took back Fort Ticonderoga, the northern fort held by the Americans since the beginning of the war. Burgoyne sent the news to King George. "I have beat them. I have beat the Americans!" crowed the king. Now that he had one victory under his belt, Burgoyne felt he was sitting pretty.

Gentleman Johnny Burgoyne liked the glamorous life. He saw no reason that war in the wilderness should change his ways. Thirty carts were devoted to carrying his precious supply of champagne, fancy dishes, and others things just for himself and his officers. Burgoyne took his time sailing down Lake Champlain from Fort Ticonderoga.

Gentleman Johnny expected General Howe's army to meet him from New York by sailing up the Hudson River. There are 23 miles separating Lake Champlain from the Hudson. At first, Burgoyne thought those 23 miles would be no problem. But those miles ran through a huge, roadless forest full of hills and rivers.

The rebels began to fight back. They blocked Burgoyne's way by felling huge trees and burning bridges. Among the men leading them was crafty old Dan Morgan with his Virginia riflemen and Benedict Arnold with his Connecticut troops.

The Iroquois started deserting Burgoyne. They didn't like being away from their homes for so long at harvest time, and they sensed that the war was going badly for the British. Without his Native American guides, Burgoyne had no way of knowing where the enemy was.

## Surrender Your Sword

Burgoyne decided that he would gather his entire army and make a stand. On October 7, 1777, the British attacked the American troops at Saratoga, New York. At first, the American response was weak. General Horatio Gates was in charge. His soldiers called him "Granny

When Generals Put Way Too Much Emphasis on Office Skills

# Turkey Gobbles and Howling Wolves

On September 19, 1777, Daniel Morgan and his men set a trap. Morgan had hidden his men in a big circle. The British redcoats thought they were alone in the woods. They heard turkeys gobbling in the woods. Well, the British *thought* they were turkeys. The gobbles were actually Morgan's signal to fire. When the British soldiers were in their line of fire,

Morgan's men pulled the triggers on their rifles, shooting first at the British officers. Morgan didn't care about 18th-century rules of conduct. General Burgoyne had to retreat. Burgoyne had to bury his dead so quickly that arms and legs were left sticking out of the ground. The British troops heard the howling of dogs and then realized it was wolves "howling over corpses . . . a hideous sound . . . as they rip it apart, the howling gets louder and louder," wrote one British soldier.

Gates." He was the kind of general who always dithered about whether to make a move or not. Gates was much better at shuffling paper than he was at leading men. In fact, he was pretty much worthless on the battlefield and even refused to leave his tent.

Luckily, Benedict Arnold was at Saratoga, too. He took over. Arnold pointed his sword at the enemy and led the charge. His horse was shot out from under him, but still he kept fighting and leading his men.

Burgoyne wrote Gates that he was willing to consider a deal. He wouldn't surrender, but he would tell his troops to lay down their arms if Gates let them all sail back to England. Gates agreed.

On October 17, 1777, in a field near Saratoga, dressed in his best uniform, Gentleman Johnny finally saw the face of his conquerors. Burgoyne wrote that he felt as if he was looking at a new race of men. When General Burgoyne gave his sword to General Gates,

Benedict Arnold was so upset by "Granny" Gates getting all the credit for the victory at Saratoga, he:

1. Learned to be a chef, eventually becoming quite famous for his eggs.
2. Went to bat for the other team.
3. Started his own United States in a parallel universe.

#2. (And we just thought it would be funny to print something upside down here.)

Gates gave it back to him as a sign of respect. Burgoyne and his troops were allowed to return to England.

## Benedict Arnold Nurses a Grudge

The guy who felt he'd gotten no respect was Benedict Arnold. Gates had stayed in his tent. Arnold had done all the fighting. Congress showered Granny Gates with medals and honors and completely ignored Arnold. Benedict Arnold wouldn't forget. Meanwhile, Gates was very happy to take all the credit. In fact, he began campaigning to have himself named the general in charge over Washington. When Gates asked Daniel Morgan to join him, Morgan yelled at him, "Under Washington and none but Washington will I serve."

## Lose a Capital and Keep on Tickin'

Gentleman Johnny would probably have never lost at Saratoga if General Howe had done what he was supposed to have done and sailed up the Hudson to combine the two British armies. But General Howe had decided that he first had to teach General George Washington a lesson for actually winning a battle at Trenton. Howe planned to march his army down to Philadelphia to take the new nation's capital. In Europe, if a nation's capital fell, the war would be over. Howe decided to capture the "head" of the rebels, their capital city. With its head gone, Howe was sure the rebellion would just wither away.

Washington tried to protect Philadelphia, but Howe had too many soldiers on his side. At Brandywine, Washington's troops took a licking. On September 26, 1777, Howe entered Philadelphia triumphantly. To Howe's disgust, however, nobody surrendered. Instead, the delegates in Congress skedaddled out of town. The Americans were fighting for their independence, not for a capital. The delegates picked up and moved to York, Pennsylvania. Congress would move nine times during the Revolutionary War.

## Valley Forge — Flags Can't Keep You Warm

At the end of 1777, the American Revolution was heading into its second winter and once again everything pretty much stopped. It was just too difficult to move men, horses, and cannons during the winter. The British held the cities of New York and Philadelphia. Burgoyne's army had been defeated at Saratoga.

Sometimes, doing that whole "honorable" thing is such a hard way to go.

# The Official Flag

Throughout he war, the rebels flew many flags, including a yellow one with a coiled rattlesnake, its forked tongue hissing. The motto on the rattlesnake flag was DON'T TREAD ON ME. Many New England troops had a white flag with a green liberty tree on it. Another flag was the Grand Union. It had 13 red and white stripes, one for each colony. In the corner were the blue-and-white crosses that were the symbol of King George III.

Finally, on June 14, 1777, Congress passed a law giving the United States of America an official flag. Flag Day is still celebrated on June 14. The law said that the United States of America was to have a red, white, and blue flag: red for courage, white for purity, and blue for justice. In the corner, there would be 13 white stars on a blue background. The stars didn't have to be in any order. Some had five points; some had six. Sometimes they were placed in a square and sometimes in a circle. Nobody knows who made the first flag. Betsy Ross is often given credit. Nearly a hundred years after the Revolution, her family claimed that she had made the first stars-and-stripes flag for General Washington. There is no proof of this.

Hi, I'm Betsy Ross. So, now you know. Maybe it wasn't me who made that first flag. But most people think it was me. I like that. You can keep a secret, right? Shhhh!

General Howe and the British army partied away with the loyalist rich folk in Philadelphia.

Washington and the Continental Army of about 11,000 wintered 22 miles northwest of Philadelphia in Valley Forge on the steep banks of the Schuylkill River. It is "a dreary kind of place," wrote Washington. The men had to build huts for themselves. Washington refused to move out of his tent and into a stone house until his men had shelter. The men were dead tired and there was no food. Over the next two days, all he ate was half a pumpkin. The men built 900 huts,

## Lots of Food, but Not for the Rebels

The irony was that the farmers in Pennsylvania had just had one of the best harvests in memory. Washington had picked Valley Forge because it was in the middle of a lush land full of flourishing farms, with cattle for meat and milk and stores of grain for bread. So why was the Continental Army starving in the midst of this plenty? The problem was money. Congress printed paper money, continental dollars, but everybody knew that the money wasn't worth the paper it was printed on. Meanwhile, the British were offering silver and gold to farmers around Valley Forge for their produce. The food was sent to Philadelphia to feed the British soldiers. Many of the Pennsylvania farmers were loyalists, anyway. They wanted Washington's army to starve and to give up the fight. And starve they did.

but the huts were cold and dank, and they had to sleep 12 to a hut.

## The Tough Get Tougher

Although 2,500 men died at Valley Forge, and another 1,000 deserted; the ones who stayed banded together. Washington needed their loyalty. Throughout the winter, there were plots and movements to remove him. Even John Adams began fretting that he had made the wrong choice. But in Valley Forge, in the frost of February, the men who survived were turning into a tough, professional army.

**Valley Forge National Historic Park** in Pennsylvania. Here you can visit the site of the Continental Army's famous winter camp. The Visitors' Center shows a film and offers maps to the major sites in the park. You can visit the house where General Washington stayed and see reconstructed huts that show what life was like for the soldiers during the winter of 1777 to 1778.

# Baron von Steuben Whips
# the Army into Shape

Baron Friedrich von Steuben from Germany showed up at Valley Forge as an unpaid volunteer. He told Washington that he had served in the Prussian army of Frederick the Great. No one knows if Baron von Steuben really was a baron and an officer. He spoke almost no English and just a little French. But of course, Lafayette spoke French and so did Alexander Hamilton. They helped von Steuben write a book about how to train an army. Von Steuben handpicked 100 men to teach first. He would stand before the shivering, half-starved soldiers in his magnificent uniform and bark out orders and curses in German. His program worked. The 100 men went on to train 100 more. By the end of the winter at Valley Forge, the soldiers who survived were in better fighting condition than they had ever been.

*I'm not sure. He's either yelling something about attack-and-evasion techniques or he's giving tips on how to make a tasty, apple-filled pastry.*

Makenize hoont arbiten spiel!

**Marie Antoinette Demonstrates Her Unfortunate Cake Fixation for Mr. Franklin**

## Vive les américains!

Meanwhile, over in France, when the news came about the victory in Saratoga, Franklin was thrilled. King Louis XVI and his young wife, Marie Antoinette, agreed to meet Franklin at their court at the Palace of Versailles. In February 1778, France formally declared itself an ally of the American rebels. Eventually, 40,000 French troops would fight in the Revolutionary War.

At first, George Washington thought that France's entering the war would mean quick victory. But the French moved slowly. Even worse, the British public, which had always been some-what sympathetic to their American cousins, suddenly were very angry. How dare the Americans make friends with their enemies, the French! Now the British prepared to attack the French on many fronts, including their islands in the West Indies. British General Howe was relieved of his duties, and Sir Henry Clinton replaced him.

Clinton was ordered to send 5,000 troops to the West Indies and to gather the remaining British force in America in New York City. Clinton left Philadelphia and marched his remaining 10,000 troops back through New Jersey.

## The Battle of Monmouth

Washington committed part of his army to leave Valley Forge and follow the British. The two armies met in Monmouth, New Jersey, on June 28, 1778, one of the hottest days of the year. The battle was a draw, with both sides taking heavy losses.

## Benedict Arnold Breaks Washington's Heart

The Battle of Monmouth was the last impor-tant engagement between the two armies in the north. For the next couple of years, neither side

# The Real Molly Pitcher

At the Battle of Monmouth, it was so hot that the soldiers were parched with thirst from the heat and stench and gunpowder. Women ran onto the battlefield and brought them water. The women were called "Molly Pitchers," because the men were yelling, "Molly, pitcher!" Mary Ludwig Hays was one of the women carrying water when she saw her husband, John, get hit. She ran to where he had been manning a cannon and tore off the bottom of her skirt to make a bandage. She took his place firing the cannon. A cannonball from the enemy went right through her petticoats. According to some accounts, the next day Washington invited Hays to his tent and told her, "You were a very brave woman. I am commissioning you a Sergeant in the Continental Army. . . . I shall call you Sergeant Molly Pitcher as the men do." Both Molly and her husband survived the Revolution. Although there were many Molly Pitchers, Mary Ludwig Hays is the one who has gone down in the history books as *the* Molly Pitcher.

"To be or not to be"? Here's your answer!

could win. The war dragged on and on. After four years of battles, with no end in sight, the Americans were getting sick of war.

Benedict Arnold was one of those who was sick and tired of the way the Revolutionary War was going. In 1779, the great hero of Fort Ticonderoga, Canada, and Saratoga married Margaret Shippen, the pretty 18-year-old daughter of an important loyalist. Peggy liked to throw big parties, and parties cost lots of money.

Arnold was angry at his country for not rewarding him with the glory and promotions that he thought he deserved. He convinced Washington to give him command of West Point, the fort that guards the Hudson River north of New York City. Arnold said he would keep it safe from the British. Meanwhile, Arnold secretly sent messages to the British that he would hand over the fort for 20,000 British pounds. British Major John André was in charge of British intelligence. By chance, André was captured with notes about Arnold's betrayal in his pocket. Arnold got wind of it and escaped just before Washington and Hamilton came to arrest him. Arnold boarded a British man-of-war and was made a general in the British army. Then he went to join the British army in the south.

# A Woman Dresses Like a Man to Fight

In 1782, Deborah Sampson (her true name was Samson, but writers misspelled it and Sampson is the way it went down on many plaques and monuments) was a teenager when the Revolutionary War began. She was about five-foot-eight, which was tall for a woman at the time. Farm work had given her broad shoulders and tough muscles. Sampson was willing to sign up for as long as the war lasted. She called herself Robert Shurtiff. She fought for a year and a half. She was wounded several times. Once she got a serious musket wound in the leg, but she wouldn't let the medics treat her because she knew they'd find out she was a woman. Finally, she got a fever, and a doctor discovered her secret. There is some historic confusion about exactly what happened next, but just as the war was ending, Robert Shurtiff was given an honorable discharge. Sampson later married and had three children.

**Deborah Sampson's Daughter Was Always Proud of Her Mom**

## Will This War *Ever* End?

By 1780, the year of Arnold's betrayal, both Congress and the states were broke. Each state printed money, but everyone knew it wasn't worth anything. The Continental Congress printed money, too. The phrase "not worth a continental" meant something was worthless. Things were moving too slowly. The French were not eager to fight. Washington's army was in a terrible position. Men who had signed up for one year kept drifting away at the end of their term. Washington desperately wanted a real army, not one made up of volunteers who could go home after 12 months. And Washington himself was tired. He had been at war now for four years. He needed new recruits, but where would they come from?

# Eggs Benedict Arnold

**General Mel:** Soldier, I entrusted you with the duty of guarding this delicious bounty from the vile claws of our dreaded enemies, the Rats. Now you have been charged with conspiring to deliver it to them for money. How do you plead?

**Prisoner Roach:** I was angry that you never gave me credit for finding that bag of day-old bagels behind the market!

**General Mel:** There is nothing that could excuse you from turning on your fellow roaches for the benefit of those "fat rats" in London!

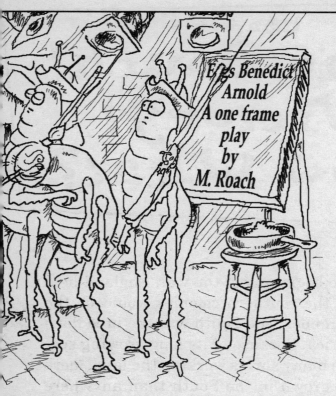

**Prisoner Roach:** But they offered me all the moldy cheese I could eat for the rest of my life.

**General Mel:** Silence! Benedict Arnold may have turned over an entire fort to his country's enemies, but this is far worse. These eggs belong to us! And you will never taste them, for your tongue works only for the enemy. As for my *loyal* soldiers . . . let them eat eggs!!

**THE END**

# Chapter 6
# The South! Victory! Now What?

**F**rom the beginning of the war, England held hopes that the southern colonies would be the first to surrender. The South was the breadbasket of America. Because of its long growing season and the many slaves working the land, more crops were grown in the South than anywhere else. The British figured if they could take the South, they could cripple and starve out the North.

TIME LINE

**1776**
British fail to take Charleston, South Carolina

**1778**
British take Savannah, Georgia

**1778–81**
British chase rebels all over the South

126

# Slaves! Fight for the King and Be Free! (Maybe)

The British knew that many colonies, such as South Carolina, had about as many slaves as white people. They thought that a slave revolt would be an easy way to conquer the South. At first, the British offered freedom to any runaway slaves, and they expected all the slaves to take them up on it. However, much as most slaves wanted freedom, it wasn't easy to run away from plantations. Runaway slaves had to travel long distances to join the British, and they risked capture and death if they were caught. Nonetheless, many African-American runaway slaves did fight for the British. However, most African Americans were not sure that the British could be trusted. They were right.

The British kept changing their minds. They took back their offer to the slaves because they discovered that too many southern loyalists were deserting them. They went back and forth on the

**1781**
British defeated at
Yorktown, Virginia

**1783**
Peace Treaty
of Paris

issue of whether African Americans should be allowed into their ranks all through the war.

In the meantime, the British attempts at starting a slave revolt convinced many southerners who had been loyal to the king to join the patriots' side. The British thought it would be easy to conquer the South. Boy, were they wrong!

## Sticky Walls

The South was host to only one major battle in the early years of the war. In June 1776, the British tried to take Charleston, South Carolina. They thought the city was full of loyalists. The British sent their mighty navy and seven regi-

I hope nobody figures out how to hit us with a wave.

**TRAVEL**

## Sullivan's Island, South Carolina.

A stone fort later replaced the log one on Sullivan's Island and served as a key defense of Charleston during the Civil War. It is named Fort Moultrie after the local commander during the Revolutionary War, Colonel William Moultrie. The Civil War–era fort still stands on the site, as well as a bunker built for World War II and a museum. A memorial describes the history of Sullivan's Island in the slave trade. There is also a beautiful view of Charleston Bay.

ments. All the patriots had in Charleston was an unfinished fort on Sullivan's Island, a barrier island in Charleston Bay. The fort looked like a kid's huge sand castle, made out of rough palmetto logs packed with the sand.

The British fired their cannons into the fort's walls. The cannonballs just sank into the soft wood. No matter how many cannonballs the British fired, most of them just stuck to the walls and didn't hurt anybody inside. The British were forced to retreat.

## The British Take Back Charleston

After their disappointing defeat in Charleston, the British did not make another major attack in the South for several years. Then in 1778, the alliance between the Americans and the French made the British think again about the South. In December 1778, the British took Savannah, Georgia, and held it for four years, despite a large naval attack by French and patriot forces in the fall of 1779.

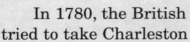

In my opinion, the large navel attack is the only way to fight a war.

In 1780, the British tried to take Charleston again. This time, they succeeded. After a long and bloody siege, the patriot commander, General Benjamin Lincoln, surrendered Charleston. It was the largest patriot defeat of the Revolution. Five thousand soldiers became prisoners, and a huge amount of weapons and artillery were lost. Lord Cornwallis was sent to hold the South.

In the spring of 1781, Cornwallis decided to push north and consolidate the southern British forces in Yorktown, Virginia. Cornwallis settled there with 8,000 soldiers, a mix of British regulars, American loyalists, and 5,000 slaves. They made camp on the York River, on the other side of the peninsula from where the first permanent British colonists had settled in Jamestown.

## Meet the Parents

### Francis "Swamp Fox" Marion (1732–1795)

Francis Marion was born along the Santee River about 45 miles from Charleston, South Carolina. He didn't look like a hero when he was born. He was so small that his parents said they could "put him in a quart jar." When he grew up, Marion was a small man with knock-knees, but he was a born leader. During the Revolution he led a group of rebels in hit-and-run guerrilla tactics that earned him the nickname "Swamp Fox." Marion and his crew would hit the enemy and then escape into the swamps.

## General Washington Rushes South

In August 1781, Washington got word that the French were going to send a fleet of 29 warships and 3,000 troops up from the West Indies. The only problem was that the ships could stay only until October 15, the start of the hurricane season. Washington knew that if he could get his troops down from New Jersey to meet them, they could trap Cornwallis. It would be a combined French and American operation to destroy Yorktown and end the war at last.

General Washington made the bold decision to march his army south to Yorktown. He fooled the commander in New York by sending spies to spread the rumor that he would attack the city from the south. Instead the troops just kept on heading south to Virginia. By the time the British commander in New York realized what Washington was doing, it was too late to stop him.

For once everything worked perfectly. The French fleet arrived on time and blockaded Yorktown from the sea. The combined French and rebel army numbered more than 16,000 men, compared to a little more than half that number fighting for the British.

Washington's troops were ready. A lot of his soldiers had deserted him, but the ones who were left were a mean fighting machine. They knew how to follow orders and to move quickly.

## Yorktown: The Surrender

The siege of Yorktown began on October 8, 1781. By October 14, the American and French were just outside the final barricades. The

Americans sent shells flying around the clock into Yorktown. The Continental Army and its French allies were ready to climb over the last barricades. The password was "Rochambeau," the name of the French general, but the Americans translated this as "Rush on Boys."

Alexander Hamilton got his soldiers to hoist him up on their shoulders; he was the first one over the final barricade. Then the battle of Yorktown turned into hand-to-hand combat with bayonets and swords.

Finally, a British officer in a red coat waved a white handkerchief. A young drummer boy was by his side. Washington signaled for his cannons to stop. Suddenly, there was silence, except for the little sound of the British drummer boys beating the surrender. "It was the most delightful music to us all," wrote one rebel. More than 8,000 British soldiers and sailors were now prisoners of war.

## Colonial National Yorktown Battlefield and Victory Center in

Yorktown, Virginia. There are museums and actual military camps that show you the daily life of a Revolutionary War soldier. Park rangers conduct tours of the siege lines. In October, the Battle of Yorktown is often re-created. You can also visit nearby **Williamsburg** and see actors portray George Washington, Patrick Henry, and Thomas Jefferson in action.

On October 19, 1781, when the British troops marched out to surrender, Lord Cornwallis stayed in his tent, claiming he was sick (almost all historians think he was lying, he just could not bear to watch). As the English surrendered, their bands played a song called "The World Turned Upside Down." Lafayette noticed that they refused to look at the Americans. So Lafayette snapped an order to his American light-infantry musicians, and they burst out playing "Yankee Doodle Dandy." British heads whipped around. That had once been *their* song, making fun of the Americans. No one was making fun of the Americans now! The British soldiers dropped their weapons on the ground and surrendered.

## Peace at Last . . . Not So Fast

Although the British still held New York and Charleston, the defeat at Yorktown ended the Revolutionary War. The head of the British Parliament, Lord North, reportedly exclaimed, "Oh, God! Oh, God! It is all over! It is all over!" when he got the bad news.

Making peace turned out to be almost as difficult as making war. Benjamin Franklin stayed in Paris. John Jay and John Adams joined him. The three of them tried to hammer out the peace agreement with the British representatives. Finally, on January 20, 1783, the peace treaty was signed in Paris. The colonies got a lot of what they asked for — and not only their independence.

England gave up its claim to all the disputed lands in the Ohio River Valley. The British representative refused to sit for a portrait after the treaty signing. When King George III heard that the treaty had been signed, he nearly choked on the word "independence." He could never stand to hear the name the "United States of America." As usual, Ben Franklin got the last word. "There's never been a good war or a bad peace," he wrote.

## I Now Take Leave of You

Finally, in November 1783, the British army sailed out of New York. Washington and his officers made a triumphant entrance into the city on horseback. Then it was time for his officers who had fought together for so long to say good-bye. On December 4, 1783, General Washington had a farewell dinner at the Fraunces Tavern, in lower Manhattan. Tears flowed faster than the rum. "With a heart full of love and gratitude, I now take leave of you," said Washington. Washington embraced each of his officers separately. Major Benjamin Tallmadge said he had never seen "such a scene of sorrow and weeping. . . . that we should see his face no more in this world seemed to me utterly insupportable." Washington was so popular that many in the new country wanted him to be king. He was offered the crown, but he

**Fraunces Tavern Museum, New York, New York.** Only the brick wall of the museum is the original, but the museum has mementoes from George Washington's farewell dinner, and downstairs you can eat in the restaurant.

refused it. Washington didn't want to be king, and he didn't want the new country to have a king. He was going back to Mount Vernon, the farm that he loved.

*No, thank ya. No, thank ya very much.*

*General Washington never liked the idea of being a king, but he really knew the job wasn't for him once he tried dressing like "The King."*

# Boy, this is fun!

The last time I got carried off on someone's shoulders was when I fell from an empty cupboard onto this woman who ran screaming out of the house.

Well, we did it. The United States of America won the war. But what do we do now? This is exactly what I was talking about just before Chapter 1. The Americans finally got their own room and now they have to figure out how to take care of it. With any luck they'll put some-

body in charge who's really messy and leaves crumbs wherever he goes. Man, that would be sweet! I'd even pay taxes for that kind of service.

One thing's for sure, George Washington was right not to want to be king. I mean, isn't that how this whole mess got started in the first place? Besides, I once knew a dog named King. He ate 17 of my best friends by accident one day just because they crawled into his food bowl to have a little snack. Kings? No thanks! But what to do? What to do . . .

# Chapter 7
# Thirteen Little States or One Big Nation?

**T**he 13 colonies were now independent. George Washington didn't want to be king. So what kind of government should take charge? Americans had to agree on a new set of rules, and everybody had an idea. Eleven states had written their own constitutions. The big question was were they going to be 13 countries or one nation?

**TIME LINE**

**1780–85**
Many northern states make slavery illegal

**1784–86**
Economic depression

**1786**
Shays' Rebellion

**1787**
Constitutional Convention

**1789**
Washington elected first President

## My Country, No, *My* Country

At the end of the Revolutionary War, there were 13 states, organized into a loose alliance by the Articles of Confederation. Under the Articles of Confederation very little got done. Nothing could be changed in the Articles without every state agreeing, and the states almost never agreed.

Yet the soldiers who had fought together side by side felt differently. Young men like Alexander Hamilton had a vision of a new, truly united country that would be a world power. Hamilton had come from nothing to be one of Washington's most trusted aides. Why shouldn't his new country rise to glory, too?

But most Americans didn't like the idea of one nation. When most people said "my country," they meant Massachusetts or "my country"

Virginia. Most people never traveled more than 30 miles from their homes. There were lots of prejudices. Most New Englanders thought all southerners were a bunch of drunken, dueling slave owners. The southerners were just as suspicious of New Englanders. They thought they were crabby and rude.

## Hey, Hey, Hey, Who's Going to Pay?

Winning a war cost money. Congress owed everybody money. The states owed everyone money. After fighting the British for so long over unfair taxes, a lot of Americans didn't like the idea of being taxed by anybody. Congress was bankrupt. After the war, the states were slipping into an economic depression. Everybody owed somebody money.

# Shays' Rebellion

In September 1786, a group of men began to stage armed protests against the state of Massachusetts. They were men who'd "bled for our country" and now they couldn't pay the mortgages on their farms. The rebellion was later named after one of its leaders, a war veteran named Daniel Shays. Shays and the other men were mostly farmers who were in debt because of the war. They wanted to force the government to help them.

Massachusetts defeated Shays' forces in January of 1787, but the rebellion scared people all over the 13 states. Some historians think that Shays' Rebellion helped speed the meeting of the Constitutional Convention because many leaders were afraid our country was falling apart.

Thomas Jefferson was not worried. He was now in France, as the United States minister. He wrote to Abigail Adams, "A little rebellion is a good thing."

# Back to the Drawing Board

At about the same time that Shays' forces were defeated in Massachusetts, Congress called for a convention to revise the Articles of Confederation. The convention was set to begin on the second Monday of May in 1787 in

FOUNDING
FATHERS
REUNION
CONCERT

Washington, Franklin,
Hamilton & Morris

BACK TOGETHER AGAIN

No flash photography or recording devices will be allow

LOST HORSE

HARPSICHORD LESSONS

LOSE WEIGH
ASK M
HOW
555-090

Philadelphia. Philadelphia was buzzing with excitement. Ben Franklin was back home and ready to greet his old friends. George Washington was coming out of retirement. Alexander Hamilton was coming as a delegate from New York as was his good friend Gouverneur Morris. Some famous leaders weren't coming, though. Jefferson was in Paris. John Adams was the United States minister in London. Patrick Henry of Virginia refused to come. "I smelt a rat," he said. Sam Adams refused to go, too. He didn't trust Hamilton.

None of the delegates knew what was going to happen when they got to Philadelphia. They didn't even call the convention a "Constitutional Convention" because they didn't yet know they were going to write a constitution.

Most of the delegates didn't get to the convention anywhere near the official first day, kind of like being two weeks late for the first day of school. It was one of the rainiest springs anyone could remember and almost every road in the 13 colonies had turned to mud. It took 11 days for enough delegates to show up to start the convention. Many of the delegates were old friends and war veterans. While they waited for the convention to start, they argued about politics and went to parties together. When George Washington arrived in Philadelphia, he headed straight to his old friend Benjamin Franklin's house for a visit and a good glass of Madeira wine.

On Friday, May 25, 1787, enough delegates had shown up to start the convention officially. The first thing the delegates did was elect George Washington the chairman of the convention. The convention needed someone who could keep order during the debates, and Washington was the most famous and respected man in the country.

When the delegates got started, they decided to keep everything that was said and written during the debates secret. Keeping the debates secret would help them to make decisions without feeling pressure from the public. They posted guards around the windows and doors of the East Room. They even nailed the windows shut to make sure no one outside heard what was said. Who knew they were going to spend the

Nail the windows shut???!!! Too bad we didn't beat the English in England. We could've been holding this convention in a big, beautiful castle.

whole long, hot summer arguing in a stuffy room with the windows closed?

## Everybody's Got a Plan

James Madison and his fellow delegates from Virginia had arrived with a plan for a new national government. They knew that whatever plan was presented first had a good chance of being considered. Their plan became known as the "Virginia Plan." The Virginia Plan called for a national government with three parts: a Congress to create law, an executive branch to enforce the law, and a judicial branch to settle arguments. The Congress would have two houses. The first house would have elected representatives. The number of representatives from each state would be based on the state's population. Then that house would elect a second house.

The small states weren't dumb. They realized that in *both* houses the big states would have much more power. Gunning Bedford from Delaware got up and said, "I do not, gentlemen, trust you. . . . Will you crush the smaller states?"

The small states came up with their own plan,

## Meet the Parents

### James Madison (1751–1836)

Most of what we know about the Constitutional Convention we know from James Madison of Virginia, who would later be both Secretary of State under Jefferson and then the fourth President of the United States. James Madison or "Little Jemmy" as he was sometimes known, was about five-foot-one with a high, squeaky voice. He was very smart: Madison knew a lot and he had read a lot.

Madison took a seat up front by his fellow Virginian, Washington. He wanted to write down everything that was said and done during the convention. "I was not absent a single day," said Madison. "Nor more than a fraction of an hour in any day." Historians will always be grateful for Madison's careful note taking. His journal gives them tons of information on what was said every single day of the convention. But, of course, we only know what Madison told us they said. Madison would not allow his notes to be published until the last delegate died. Guess who it was? James Madison himself. He died in 1836 when he was 85.

which became known as the "New Jersey Plan." The New Jersey Plan called for a one-house Congress where each state had an equal number of votes. This would give small states the same voice as large ones in the new national government.

**The Quickly Rejected "Pie à la Mode" Plan**

## The Great Compromise

The delegates argued for weeks and weeks. Big states, small states, one house, two houses? It was a hot summer and tempers were getting just as hot. Finally, they came up with a compromise. In the Senate, all states would be equal. Even the smallest state would get two senators. But in the House of Representatives, representation would be based on population, and there would be a census every 10 years to count the people. And that is the system we still have today. The Great Compromise put the convention back on track. Now the delegates had to try to settle some other problems. They decided there would be a single president elected every four years by the electoral college, and a Supreme Court to decide disputes.

Counting everybody in a country is . . .

| EASY | NOT EASY |

## How Can I Be Three-fifths of a Person?

Slavery was still legal in most of the states, although several northern states had started to make it illegal. Many of the leaders of the Revolution had turned against slavery because they saw how bravely the African Americans had fought with them. In New York City, Alexander Hamilton had started a society to free slaves. Gouverneur Morris said that slavery was "the curse of heaven. . . . Are they men? Then make them Citizens and let them vote." George Washington rewrote his will to free his slaves when he died.

The delegates settled their argument about population with a strange compromise: The southern states could count each slave as three-fifths of a person. Five hundred slaves would

## Call It Anything but Slavery

Our Constitution is mostly written in clear and beautiful English. But when it came to slavery it was as if the constitutional writers were embarrassed to use the word. The word "slave" is never mentioned. The writers thought of every other way to put it, such as "person held to service or labor," or "all other persons." Later, during the Civil War, President Abraham Lincoln would say "the word 'slavery' was hid away in the Constitution just as an afflicted man hides away a cancer which he dares not cut out at once, lest he bleed to death."

count the same as 300 free citizens in the population count of each state. The delegates also allowed the southern states to continue importing slaves for another 20 years. The delegates who hated slavery had decided to delay their fight. They thought that dealing with it at that time might destroy the chances for a national government to exist at all.

## A New President for a New Nation

"We the People of the United States." When the Revolution began, those words wouldn't have made any sense. After a long hard war, they did. There was a new nation filled with people who had chosen to stay united. There was still a lot of

# We the People

When the final compromises had been made, the whole Constitution was given to a committee on style to whip it into shape. Gouverneur Morris was known to be the best writer, so the committee gave the job to him. He was just supposed to check the spelling and grammar. The draft he was given read, "We the people of the states of North Carolina, Virginia, Massachusetts," etc.

Morris changed it to *"WE the People of the UNITED STATES, in Order to form a more perfect Union, establish Justice, ensure domestic Tranquility, provide for the common Defence, promote the general Welfare and secure the Blessings of Liberty to ourselves and our Posterity do ordain and establish this CONSTITUTION of the United States of America."*

Hooray for forming "perfect unions"! Like strawberries and chocolate. Sun and sea. Kids and kittens. Milk and cookies.

work to be done. One of the first jobs was to put in a Bill of Rights that would outline the basic freedoms that Americans felt they had fought the war to get. They were freedoms protecting individual

**TRAVEL**

liberties from government restrictions. The Bill of Rights spell out freedom of speech, freedom of religion, freedom of the press, the right to assemble and protest, the right to bear arms, the right to a speedy trial, and protection from unreasonable searches and seizures.

On February 4, 1789, George Washington was elected the first President of the United

States of America. Not one single electoral vote was cast against him. Nobody knew exactly where to put the capital of the new nation, so they decided to put it temporarily in New York City. At noon on April 30, 1789, George Washington took the oath of office on the balcony of Federal Hall, overlooking Wall Street. The ceremony almost had to be delayed because nobody had remembered to bring a Bible and they had to search through nearby bookstores and houses to find one. But they did, and Washington put his left hand on the Bible and raised his right. He said the words that had been written into the Constitution. They are still said today as each president takes office. "I do solemnly swear that I will faithfully execute the Office of President of the United States and will to the best of my ability, preserve, protect, and defend the Constitution of the United States." Washington uttered four words of his own — "so help me God" — which every president since has repeated. Then the crowd roared, "Long live George Washington, President of the United States." There was a huge parade to celebrate the event. The baby country was going to try to go it alone without a "mother." Would it ever survive? Nobody knew what would happen next.

# Well, there you

have it: a new president, a new nation, and a brand-new way of running things. And more than 200 years later, we still do it the same way! Of course, these days women and African Americans have the right to vote just like anybody else. No more of that "three-fifths of a person" junk. Boy, that idea smelled so bad even I wouldn't go near it!

So, in closing, I'd like to take this opportunity to thank all the good people who made this country possible. First, George Washington, without whose support and heroism I wouldn't be standing before you today. Thomas Jefferson for writing so good . . . sorry, that's writing so *well*. Let's see, there's also Benjamin Franklin who taught me the benefits of an air bath. And Mercy Otis Warren for making me laugh, and Deborah Sampson, who showed us all that clothes make the man, er, the woman . . . well, whatever.

There are just so many people to thank, but it looks like I'm running out of time (or pages, to be precise). So let me just wrap it up by thanking *you* for reading along with me and learning all about how our great country came to be.

Bye-bye for now!

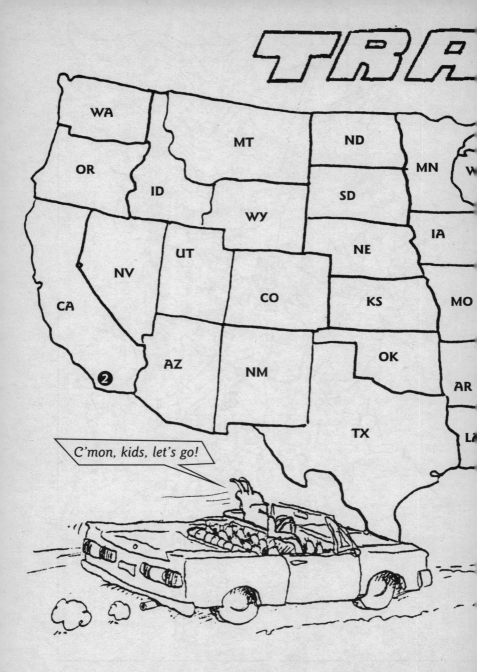

VEL

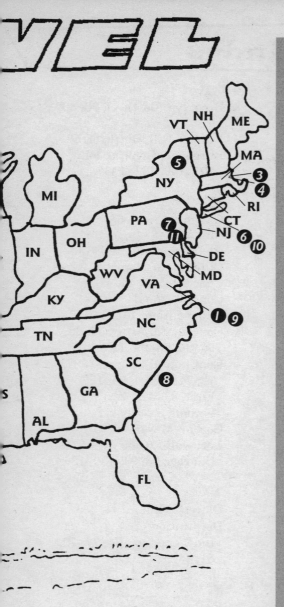

# Index